Growing up in
EDWARDIAN BRITAIN

Nance Lui Fyson

B. T. Batsford Ltd *London*

The Illustrations

Contents

© Nance Lui Fyson 1980
First published 1980

Printed by Garden City Press,
Letchworth, Herts.
for the Publishers B T Batsford Limited
4 Fitzhardinge Street, London W1H 0AH

ISBN 0 7134 3372 8

Date List

1900 Conservatives win General Election, with Lord Salisbury as PM
1901 Queen Victoria dies. Edward VII becomes King
1902 Salisbury resigns. A.J. Balfour succeeds as Conservative PM
      Education Act ends School Boards, puts elementary and secondary education under control of county borough councils
      Peace of Vereeniging — end of the Second Boer War
1903 First Garden City established (Letchworth)
      Women's Social and Political Union starts (to become focus of campaign for votes for women)
1905 Prime Minister Balfour resigns (Dec.)
1906 (Jan.) Liberals win General Election, with Campbell-Bannerman as PM
      Local authorities start free school meals for needy children
      Larger grants offer for secondary schools on condition they offer 25 per cent free places
1907 First Boy Scout camp, with Baden-Powell
      School authorities required to medically inspect children
1908 Asquith takes over as Liberal Prime Minister
      Children Act set up separate courts for children, minimum prison age raised to fourteen
1909 Old Age Pensions begin (for those over seventy with less than ten shillings a week income and no criminal record)
1910 (Jan.) General Election, Liberals returned
      (Dec.) Another General Election, Conservatives barely in
      Kind Edward VII dies (May), George V becomes King
1911 Balfour resigns as Conservative leader, replaced by Bonar Law
      Lloyd George (Chancellor) introduces National Insurance Act
      Wave of strikes, including children's school strikes
1912 *Titanic* (world's largest ship) sinks
1914 (June) Archduke of Serbia is shot, leading to outbreak of First World War (4 August)
      Irish Home Rule Bill is passed by Commons, but suspended until after the war
1915 Liberal MP Asquith forms coalition cabinet, including Conservatives and Labour
      Many counties lower school-leaving age so more children can work to aid war effort
1916 (Dec.) Lloyd George succeeds Asquith as PM of the coalition government
      National Service Act starts military conscription
1918 End of war (November)
      Education Act raises school-leaving age to 14
      Unemployment Insurance made universal, "dole" introduced
      Parliamentary vote extends to all men over 21, and women over 30 with some property
      (Dec.) General Election returns Lloyd George as head of post-war coalition government

1 The Edwardian Era

The Edwardian era began in 1901 when King Edward VII came to the throne, already nearly sixty years of age. He was somewhat less stern and more pleasure-loving than his mother, Queen Victoria, had been. His friends' children raced slices of hot buttered toast along the stripes of his trousers and called him "Kingy".

Edwardian Britain followed the King's lead. New inventions (in transport, communications, etc) provided more possibilities for leisure and entertainments. And for the small number of rich, this was certainly an age of good living.

But of a total population of 33 million in 1901, only one million earned even enough to pay income tax, which was levied on incomes of £160 a year and more. About one third of the population lived in real poverty. Fred Hillsdon (b.1906):

> The poverty was terrible. It taught us all you had to go scrounging. You were fighting to try and live.

Poorest of all, the bottom one or two per cent, were those in what were called "workhouses" or "unions". These over-crowded places of charity gave rough shelter to the very poor, sick and old, in exchange for work. They were seen as a degrading last resort. Very poor children too ended up in workhouses.

The Liberal Party, having won the General Election of 1906, brought in a few social reforms which began, slowly, to build the welfare state in Britain. The idea was that the whole community, instead of shunning the poor, should contribute more towards helping the old, the sick and the less well-off. The old age pension, introduced in 1909, and the National Health Insurance Act (1911) were small steps towards making this idea reality.

Still, the social classes were sharply divided. The middle and upper classes were inclined to say that the poor were to blame for their own poverty. And the working classes in early Edwardian times mostly accepted their lot. Trade Unions had very little power to improve wages and working conditions in the early 1900s. However, by 1911 discontent began to show in a wave of strikes and violence, and in the few years before the outbreak of the First World War there was much unrest.

Women joined in the growing protests. The suffragettes campaigned increasingly for the right of women to vote. By 1914 their tactics, which had included hunger strikes and chaining themselves to railings, escalated to setting fire to public buildings and smashing exhibits in national museums. Only in 1918 was the right to vote extended to all adult men, and to some women (those over 30 years old who owned some property).

Struggle was taking place over Ireland. From the turn of the century a variety of extreme Irish nationalist movements were continuing demands for an independent Irish Republic. In 1912 a Home Rule Bill did propose a separate Parliament for Ireland. But the Ulster Protestant minority

wanted to stay part of Britain. The Irish nationalists did not want Ireland divided (part independent, part British) as it is today. The disagreement was leading to civil war which was only postponed, as was Home Rule, until after the First World War.

Change affected all aspects of life. People and ideas could move about much more and much faster. As more and more people migrated to the towns and cities, country crafts and traditions began to lose ground. The industrial development of Victorian times had turned Britain from a rural into

1   An Edwardian city street market, 1904. Britain was then the most urbanized country in the world. By 1911 less than one quarter of the population lived in rural areas, and only 7 per cent of the workforce were in farming.

2 and 3   Poor children in 1912 and rich children ➤ in 1903. The contrast between rich and poor children was striking. Rowntree's 1901 survey of poverty in York found 28 per cent of the people (and closer to 40 per cent of the children) without the bare essentials of life, such as enough food. (Using his same standards, only 2 per cent of York was so poverty-stricken by 1950.)

4   Children loyally wave their flags for Empire Day, 1913. Between 1884 and 1900 Britain had colonized some 3,750,000 square miles of overseas land, and some 50 million overseas people. British children were taught to be proud of the expanded empire. But the cost of maintaining forces for the empire and investment overseas meant that not enough was spent on updating industry at home.

an urban society — and further urbanization went on during Edward's reign.

Britain's role in the world changed too. Although Britain still commanded a large overseas empire, the British in the 1900s could no longer feel (as they had in the 1870s) that they were the richest and most powerful nation on earth. Britain in 1914 was the largest exporter of manufactured goods, but her share of world trade was already declining. Other countries — Germany, the United States — rose in competition.

On a May morning in 1910 headmasters all over Britain announced to schoolchildren that King Edward VII had died. The children said a prayer and looked forward to the coronation of King George V. Although Edward's reign ended in 1910 the "Edwardian era" is taken to include the extra years until the start of the First World War in 1914. It was the coming of war which marked the end of the era.

2 Transport and Communications

Great changes were noticed in transport and communications in the early 1900s. By 1901 letters could be posted to places all over Britain for the standard rate of one penny. The telegraph was well established and there were cables to send messages overseas. The telephone had been invented but was yet to come into general use. The network of railways was being improved. In 1903 the first motor-driven aircraft was flown in America by the Wright brothers. (The flight lasted only 59 seconds at a speed of 30 miles (48 km) per hour.) Steamers replaced sailing-ships. The last great sailing-ship was built in 1906.

As always, people were often wary of the changes. In 1911 a moving staircase (escalator) was installed at Earls Court station. A man with a wooden leg was hired to ride up and down to prove its safety! (Moving, electric staircases were not common in underground stations before the First World War.)

Electric vehicles

The introduction of electricity made the tube trains possible. London's Bakerloo Line was opened in 1906 and the under-

5 1912. Going on a school outing. While new forms of transport were spreading, horse-drawn vehicles were still used. In 1912 over 500 hansom cabs still moved about London. Small traders used horses, as did the breweries.

6 1909. Dancers arrive by motor bus at Cumberland Market. Just as electric trams replaced horse-drawn trams in early Edwardian years, so the motor bus came to largely replace electric trams later on in the period. By 1913 there were some 3,000 motor buses in London.

ground railway was first joined to the over-head system in 1913.

All-electric tramcars had come into use in cities in the late 1890s and early 1900s. The great mass of children and their parents

then had the chance to travel much more throughout the cities. Journeys on the tramcars were only about half the cost and twice as fast as on the old horse-drawn trams.

Motor vehicles

In just the same way as railways in Victorian times had been a tremendous new thing, so the recently invented motor car during Edward's reign became enormously popular. In 1890 the working classes had travelled mostly by walking. By 1920 not only were they using public transport, but also a relatively cheap motor car was available to them. The bicycle too had become popular over this time.

Motor cars were actually running on British roads as early as in 1894, but only in small numbers. They were extremely

7   1908. Motor cars were only for the rich in early Edwardian times. But in 1908 the era of the popular, cheaper car began with imports of the Ford. By 1910 there were over 100,000 motor cars registered in Britain.

expensive and constantly breaking down. Motorists were very unpopular with their noise and fumes, and were accused of frightening the horses.

Despite such early suspicion and dislike, motor cars soon became more widespread. In 1903 the speed limit was raised from 14 to 20 miles (24 to 32 km) per hour. In the same year the first experimental motor bus appeared in London. By 1911 the last horse-drawn bus was withdrawn from London streets and only motor buses were used from then on.

By 1913 it was reported that England had some 220,000 licensed motor vehicles. This was twice as many as any country in Europe, but only one third of the number in America. The first time that Edith Storry even saw a motor car was at the age of 13 in 1907:

My sister used to work for a photographer. He gave us a ride one Sunday morning. He took us five mile out. When I come back I said it seems as though I been miles and miles.

3 Family Life

Helping in the house

Children helped out in many Edwardian homes by doing all sorts of jobs. As a child in Wales, Albert Edwards (b.1904) would go out on the slag heaps picking coal. By the age of eight he was fetching home a heavy sackload. "We used to go and get what we could for warmth, firewood and that." Another job was sweeping horse-dung off the road into buckets, fetching it home for the garden.

Florence Goddard (b.1892) cleaned the knives ("real steel knives they were in those days") and the shoes. Edith Storry (b.1894) in about 1905 used to help make rugs for the fireside. Old clothes were used, cut into pieces all about the same length. Children aged eight and nine washed up, cleaned floors, washed windows. Those living on farms helped with such jobs as feeding and watching animals, or picking potatoes.

Well-off families

On the other hand, children of better-off families with servants took little part in the home. Margaret and Pam Steven (b.1911 and 1908) lived on the nursery floor at the top of the house:

8 A mother and boy in the Shetlands in the early 1900s. Crofters' children joined in the conversation and social life of adults. This was the one area of Britain where physical punishment of children was not common. There were fewer rules for children, and crofters' children were generally treated much more as equals by their elders.

You could look right down to this hall at the bottom of the stairs. We used to love to look over the banisters and see what was going on. We were kept so much out of it all.

For children like Margaret and Pam, a nanny lived on the nursery floor to look after them.

We only went downstairs after tea to see Mummy and any friends she had there, which she always seemed to have. We were all poshed up to go downstairs for about half an hour at the most and shown off and then back to the nursery. Mummy and Daddy always came up to kiss us good night. Occasionally we were terribly lucky and taken out for a walk with them or even allowed to go trotting about on the golf course while they played golf. It was a tremendous treat.

Discipline

For all children, rich and poor, parents, and especially fathers, were to be obeyed and respected. Some homes were much

9   1911. A nursemaid and her charges in Hyde Park. Rich children were often distant from their parents, seeing them only for a short time each day and perhaps for longer on Sundays. A closer attachment might be to "nanny".

more easy-going than others, some parents much stricter than others. Many children were in real fear of their parents and adults in general. Discipline could be very harsh. An advert for Quaker Oats showed a drawing of a father beating his small son across his bare bottom with the back of a hairbrush. The text read: "THE MORE PAINS-TAKING THE PROCESS the more certain the results . . ."

For better-off children like Margaret and Pam Steven (b.1911 and 1908) it was often nanny who disciplined them. At the age of six, Pam Steven was put in the box room for some deed:

The box room was a dark attic, no light at all. Nothing except old trunks. It was on the nursery floor. I was shut in there in the dark until nanny considered I was good enough to come out.

13

In most homes the father had the authority. Teenagers, and especially girls, were usually under close control. Fathers laid down at what time they were to be in, and beating could be the punishment for being only a few minutes late. Edith Storry (b.1894) was the youngest of seven children. In the early 1900s her older sisters were engaged but not allowed out after ten o'clock at night:

If they were five or ten minutes late my father was waiting with a leather strap, strap the back of their hands.

Men

Husbands in well-off Edwardian households did no work in the house. Servants did everything. In most working-class families, too, husbands did little housework, mainly because they were working such long hours outside the home. But there were certainly a number of working-class and middle-class homes where husbands helped as they could.

Women

Only about one in ten married women were in paid work in Edwardian times. (The

10 1906. Edwardian girls generally left school earlier and married later than young women today. About 20 per cent remained permanently single, compared to only 5 per cent now. The average age of starting menstruation (so being able to bear children) was 15, compared to 13 in the 1960s.

11 1914. A family with some of its 19 children. Average family size was already down to three or four children in Edwardian times — although there were still much larger families.

12   1901. Only about 25-30 per cent of Edwardian families attended church on a Sunday, but most Edwardians still regarded themselves as belonging to some religion. The church still baptized more than two thirds of all babies, and more than two thirds of weddings were held in church. More people went to church in the countryside than in the cities.

figure was more than five in ten in the 1980s.) And one third of those Edwardian women who did outside work were domestic servants. Compared with women in the 1980s, Edwardian women married at an older age, bore more children, and died younger.

Family size
Three or four children was the average size of Edwardian families. Families in Victorian times had been larger still, with an average of six children for couples married in the 1860s. While there were still many large families, more and more Edwardians were having just two children. And so a growing number of parents had more chance to give individual time and attention to each child.

Marriage
Edwardian couples marrying in 1911 had an average of 28 years before them. (Those marrying in the 1980s could expect nearly 45 or 50 years together.) Because people, on average, lived shorter lives, it was much less common for Edwardian children to have their grandparents alive than it is for children in the 1980s. In 1901 only 4 per cent of the population was over 65 years old, whereas in the mid-1970s 16 per cent were 65 and older.

Divorce was still rare, except among the very rich, but many couples were separated. Undoubtedly too, the parents of many Edwardian children stayed together unhappily.

4 Housing

With orange boxes for furniture and old coats as bedding, the very poorest Edwardian children lived with their families in damp single rooms. Many were underground basements, with no windows or ventilation. The only water might have been from a tap in the yard.

In 1911 nearly 10 per cent of British people were still in over-crowded housing (more than two people to one room). This was less than 2 per cent in the 1970s.

Edwardian Scotland had fully half its population in over-crowded conditions. About half of Scottish housing were homes of just one or two rooms. Tenement flats

13 London, 1912. In 1914 Birmingham still had 40,000 houses without any drainage or water taps. It was the unhealthiest of the large English cities. But London was even worse for over-crowding: more than one sixth of London people were in housing with more than two people to a room.

were common in towns.

There was more really bad housing in Edwardian times, but there were also, at the other extreme, some very grand houses indeed. Extremely rich children might have lived in a country house with more than one hundred rooms and over fifty servants to run it. And that would have been only one of several houses run by the family.

However, under 10 per cent of Edwardian families had even one living-in servant. For children of a typical working man, home in the early 1900s was likely to be a stone or brick terrace house, with a parlour, lean-to scullery leading to a small back garden, and three bedrooms upstairs. Children often slept two, three, or more in a bed. Teenage boys and girls sometimes had to share a bedroom, with just a curtain dividing the area.

In reasonably well-off homes the kitchen might have had linoleum on the floor, a table and chairs, and a dresser. Besides the open fire and oven in the kitchen, there might have been a gas stove in the scullery. The parlour would have been used mainly

14 1912. Ninety per cent of housing was private landlord-owned before 1914 (compared to about 13 per cent in the 1980s). The houses were not kept in good condition. Newspapers still reported children being bitten to death by rats. Thousands more Edwardians were quite homeless. They slept in tents, barns, or doorways.

on Sundays and for visitors. It might have been furnished with a sofa and small table, piano, perhaps some stuffed birds, china ornaments, and lace curtains at the window.

Housing in the industrial north

Houses in northern industrial towns were generally smaller than in southern English towns. Often they had just two or three bedrooms above, and front and back kitchens on the ground floor. The front kitchen was really a living-room, with the cooking range in it. The back kitchen was the larder and wash-house. The back yard would have held a rough privy and a pit for refuse. In some places there was not even a yard. More than one quarter of these northern town houses had no drainage. Excrement from the privies was periodically shovelled out into barrows by workmen. These barrows were then emptied into carts in the street.

Housing in country areas

Country housing in both England and Scotland consisted mostly of cottages with no more than two bedrooms. Damp brick or earth floors were still common. There was no drainage, collection of refuse, or running water in rural areas. Water came from wells or streams. Albert Edwards (b.1904 in Wales) was the youngest of thirteen children:

We used to catch our water from the roof, in tubs outside. We didn't have no taps then. We used to have a well but mostly all the water we used was rainwater. For drinking water we had natural water coming down from the mountainside. We used to have a big jack and carry all our drinking water. That's why my arms are so long as they are now, is carrying them things as a kid. We had to go up there first thing in the morning, carrying the jack. There wasn't flush toilets and that in them days. The toilet was out the back, they weren't indoors. You never thought it was possible to have a toilet indoors.

Fitted bathrooms were, however, becoming common in better-off homes in towns and cities.

The simplest country houses in Britain were probably the "black houses" in the crofting counties of Scotland. These were built of stones by the crofters. They had thick walls, roof rafters made of driftwood, and a thatched roof of barley straw tied with heather. A peat fire in a ring of stones burned in the middle room. In one end room the family slept in box-beds. The other end room housed the cattle in winter. With wet mud for a floor (the roof always leaked) and just planks and boxes for furniture, these were very simple homes

15 1912. There is a single gas-ring for cooking ➤ **next to the fire. Electricity was still used only in public places and in private homes of the well-to-do. Gas for cooking and lighting was more generally available.**

indeed. In some counties, including Argyll, Orkney, and Shetland, two-roomed cottages had mostly replaced the black houses.

Babies were much more likely to survive in Scotland than in the mill or mining towns of England. A baby born in a London workhouse had about the worst chance of all.

Gas and electricity

For Albert Edwards (b.1904 in Wales) and Edmund Dalton (b.1909 in Ireland) and most other Edwardian children, lighting in the house was by oil lamp and candles. Usually the sitting-room was the only room of a house to have an oil lamp. People took candles with them to light their way to the bedrooms.

During Edwardian times gas and electric light replaced oil lamps in better-off homes in city areas. The early electric carbon bulbs were not very good and people often preferred the clearer light of gas lamps.

A variety of new inventions were slowly coming into Edwardian homes to make housework and cooking easier. The first Ideal Home Exhibition was held in 1908. Early gas ovens and electric fires and kettles were among the displays. A great novelty, still only for the rich, was a vacuum cleaner small enough for one person to use. (Carpets were still mainly hand-swept by kneeling maids.)

Keeping warm

Heating was mainly by coal and wood fires. The poor could rarely afford to buy coal. What they had was mostly that picked up by children, or stolen, or even taken from

16 1910. Pianos were an important piece of ➤ **furniture in middle-class homes and in working-class homes that could afford them. Singing round the piano was a popular home entertainment.**

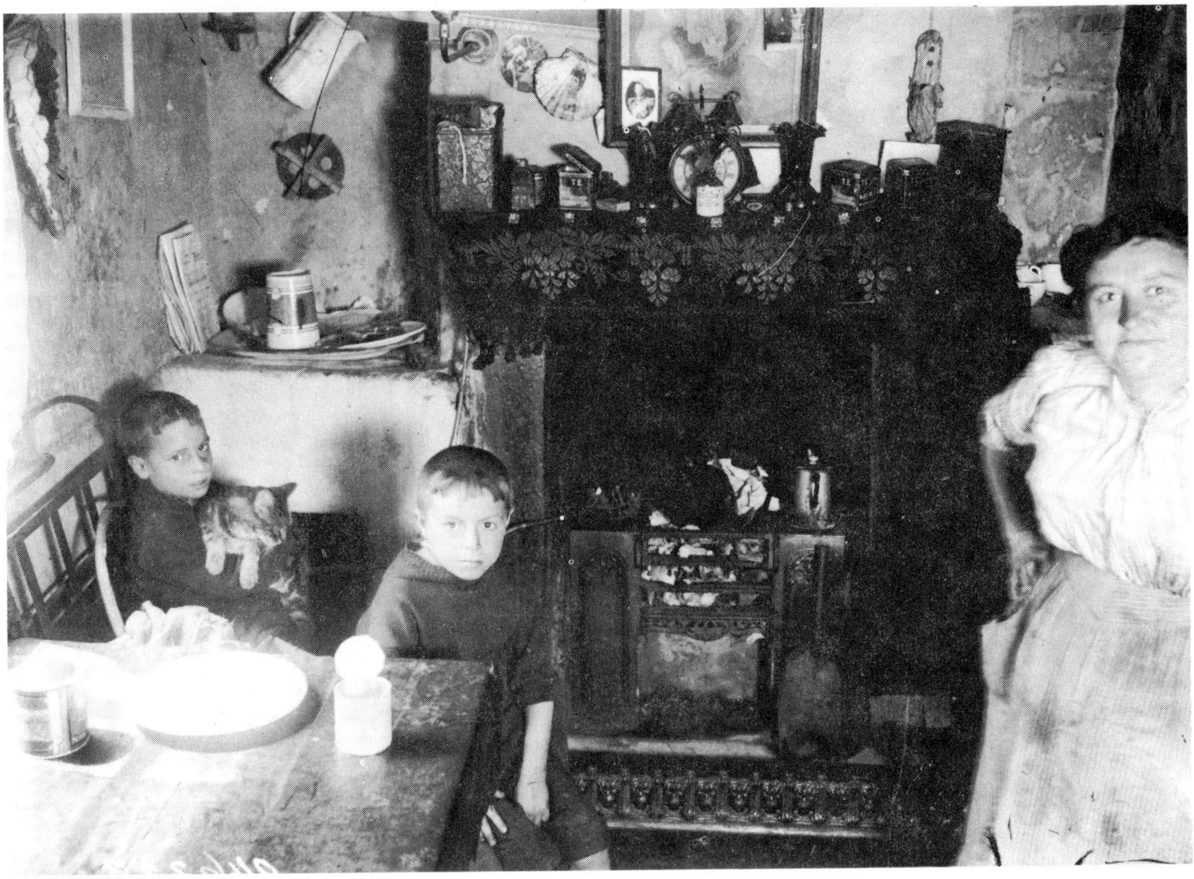

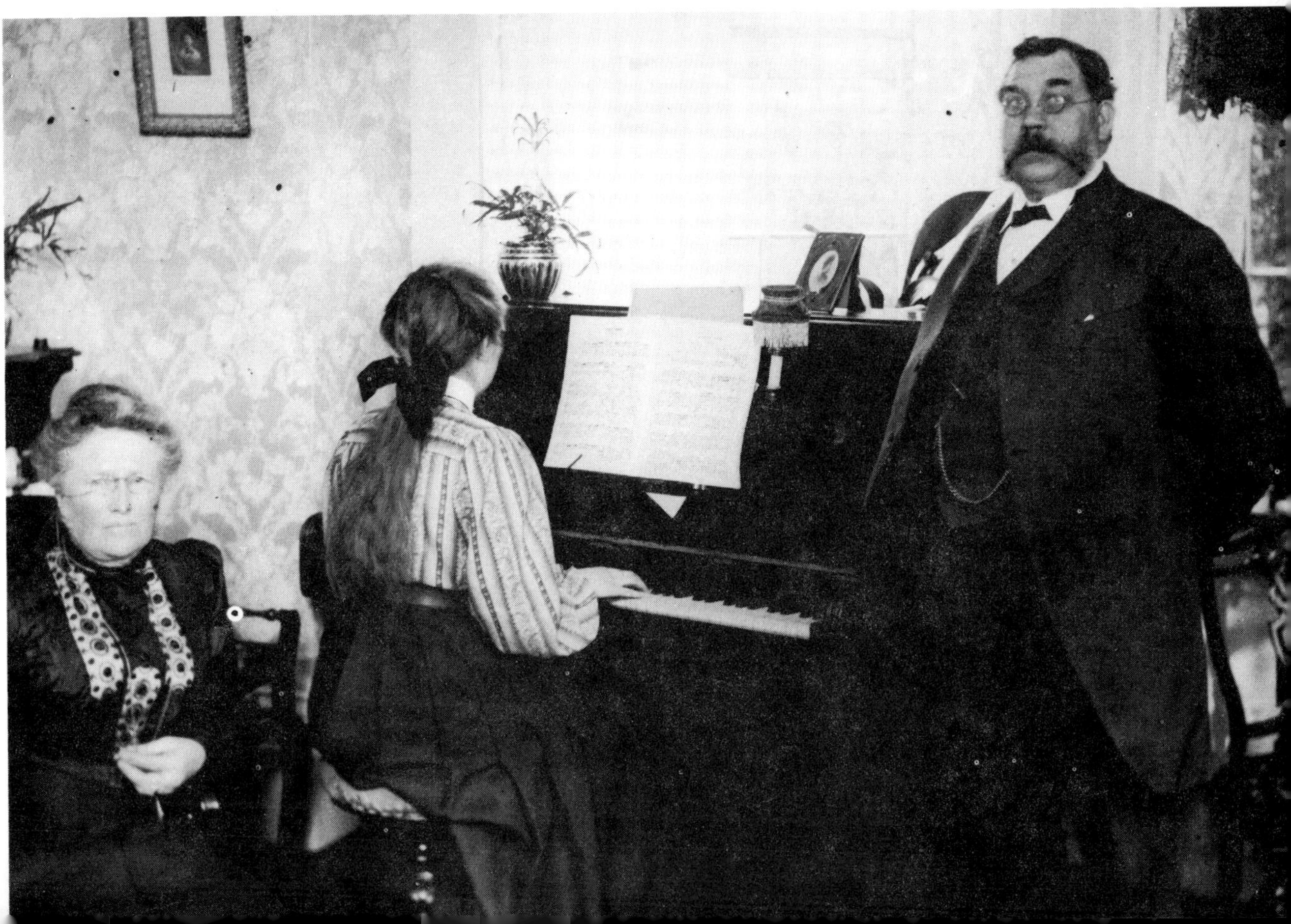

canals which were dragged for what barges had dropped.

In richer homes fires were lit and looked after by maids. Pam and Margaret Steven (b.1908 and 1911) had stone hot-water-bottles. There were small ones for children and tiny ones for babies' cots.

The Steven sisters in about 1914 secretly crept up the back stairs to have a look at where the servants slept:

We were never allowed to go up there. I've never forgotten it. There were about four large rooms with bare boards and a tiny rug by the side of each bed, with double beds in each room. There was a washstand with a basin in it and an iron bedstead and that's all there was. It was cold and draughty.

New building

In 1898 a book called *Tomorrow* by Ebenezer Howard was published. Howard put forward the idea that cities should be built in open country, to combine the advantages of urban and rural life. These new cities of not more than 30,000 people were to include workshops and factories so that the inhabitants would not need to travel a long distance to work. The first "Garden City" was built at Letchworth in 1903, and the idea of town planning took root. Hampstead Garden Suburb, which was started in 1907, extended an area already built up.

Improved public transport encouraged the building up of the suburbs. The new suburban houses built between 1901 and 1910 went mainly to office workers, for whom there was a great new demand in the towns. One style favoured for the houses in these suburbs was based on the ideas of William Morris. He wanted a return to more hand-produced, craft goods. Real hand-crafted goods were becoming beyond the means of most people, but they could afford the mass-produced imitations of old styles. For example, wooden slats were nailed to house fronts to look like old styles of timber-framing. "Bulls-eyes" were put into window glass, copying what had actually been a fault in the work of early glass-makers. Small windows with leaded lights were popular.

Generally, better-off Edwardian children lived in rather lighter and more comfortable houses than children in Victorian times. The less heavy furniture gave more room to move, and real flowers were more often on display. Kitchens were no longer put into basements in newly built homes. White paint was more common, and there was white or green painted furniture for children's rooms.

5 Health

17 1910. This baby looks very well. Some rich babies were doped with opium by their nurses to keep them quiet. And many fretful poorer babies too were given "Mother's Friend" (known as "knockout drops") with tincture of opium. Most Edwardian babies were breast-fed, except in areas such as the cotton towns where working mothers found this difficult.

Every week in 1903 about six thousand children were born in Greater London. One thousand of these did not live to be even one year old. In the middle-class suburbs about 96 per cent of infants would survive their first year. But in the slums as many as one baby in three would die.

Of the children who did celebrate their first birthday, those in middle-class neighbourhoods could expect to live, on average, about 50 years. By comparison, life expectancy was just 36 years in working-class areas. (British children born in the 1980s have an average life expectancy of well over 70 years.)

The medical department set up by the Board of Education in 1907 examined schoolchildren and found ready evidence of poor health. Many children were found to be undernourished, verminous, with bad teeth and poor eyesight. Those from overcrowded homes weighed an average of ten pounds less and were five inches shorter than those from reasonable housing.

Health standards did improve steadily over the Edwardian period. While 30 per cent of London children were found flea-bitten in 1908, the figure was under 4 per cent by the 1920s. The spread of indoor water taps, making it easier for families to keep clean, was an important factor in health improvement.

Illnesses

Children's diseases of the time included small-pox, whooping-cough, typhus fever, enteric fever, scarlet fever and diphtheria. Pam Steven (b.1908):

> Scarlet fever was very serious then. It was the thing everyone was very frightened of.

It was common to find a school's log-book noting "with sorrow" the death of a child, perhaps aged only ten, from a disease like pneumonia.

Medical care

Poorer families could not often afford to call a doctor or dentist. For Albert Edwards (b.1904 in Wales) the solution for tooth-ache was to tie a string to the tooth, tie the string to the door, "slam the door and pull it out that way".

In 1911 the National Health Insurance Act laid down that every working person should contribute towards health insurance. The insured worker then did not have to pay doctor's bills, and sickness benefit

18 A cleansing station, 1912. Edwardian school inspectors in poorer areas found whole classes infected with head-vermin and many with body-lice. As many as one quarter of a class might have been barefoot. A larger number had bow legs, caused by the vitamin deficiency disease rickets. Some had open sores.

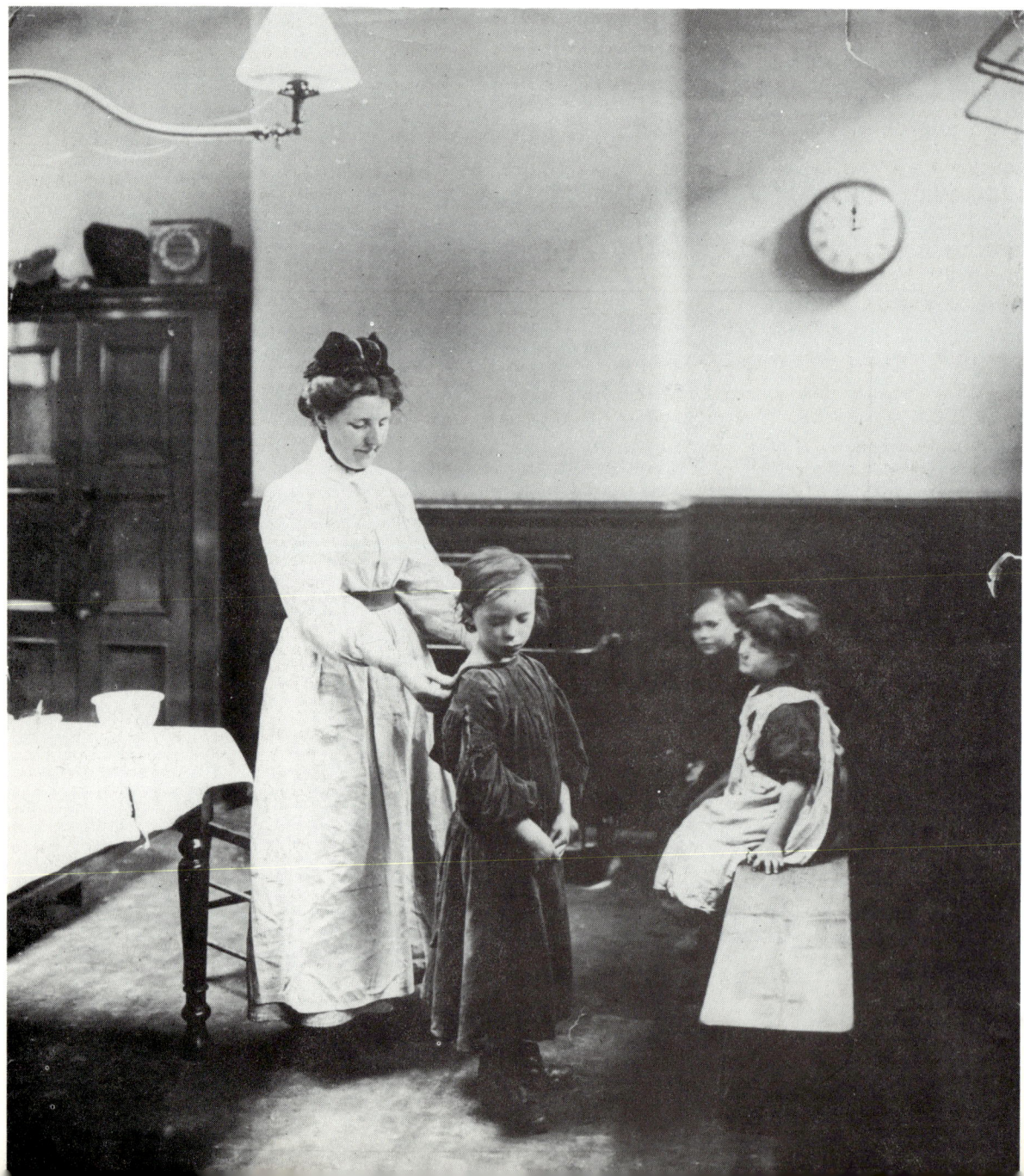

would be paid to him if he was away from work through illness. But this insurance did not yet cover the worker's whole family as it does today.

Hospitals were still fairly crude places, despite the progress made in the nineteenth century in the understanding of infection. X-rays, which had been discovered only in 1895, were a new aid in Edwardian years.

Public infirmaries developed besides those which were part of workhouses. These new infirmaries offered some free treatment without people feeling that they were being labelled "paupers".

Local authorities did more health work. There were more clinics, and more milk schemes for babies. After 1909 the Local Government Board put much pressure on authorities to deal with health matters. As more homes were changing from privies to water closets, so general water and sewage schemes improved. Such improvements meant that many more babies and children would survive.

19 Christmas at the Hospital for Sick Children. The nurse brings the patient a doll. The number of hospital beds was increasing in Edwardian times, but the middle class still preferred to be nursed and even operated on at home.

Medicine

Medicines, and quack medicines, were widely advertized in the popular press and bought in chemist's shops. Constipation was one common complaint for which parents regularly dosed not only themselves but also their children. Flo Connors (b.1901) was given a laxative "every Friday night after we had a bath in front of the fire."

She was one of eight children, who would all take it in turns to use the same washing bath. "The girls would go first and then the boys." About three or four would use the same water, then it was changed.

For Margaret and Pam Steven (b.1911 and 1908), who, incidentally, had a bath every day, going on holiday was spoilt by the hated dose of medicine:

When you went to the seaside you were given a dose of syrup of figs the night you arrived. It was a dark brown liquid that tasted foul — a sort of laxative. You had to have your nose held and somebody opened your mouth and poured it down. The night you got home from holiday you got another one.

Castor oil was also commonly given to children.

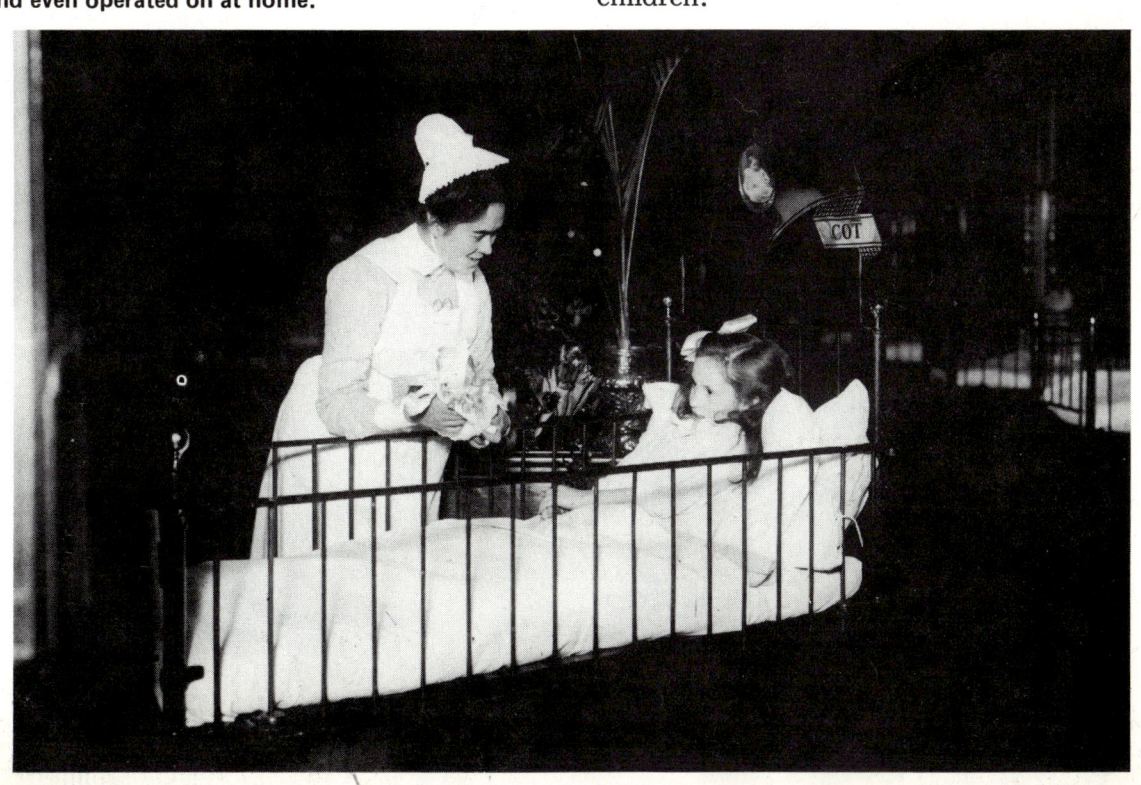

6 Food and Drink

"Tum-Tum" was a nickname for King Edward VII — who did indeed like the pleasures of food and women. For rich Edwardians heavy eating and elaborate menus were common. A 1902 survey showed that upper-class families ate three times as much meat, four times as much milk, and three times as much butter as working-class families. Twelve year-olds at public schools were an average of five inches taller than those at state schools!

Upper-middle-class and rich children

In one typical upper-middle-class family the children ate with their parents on Sundays only. Usually children had their meals in the nursery with their nurse, while other servants ate in the kitchen. The midday meal for the children might have been "a boar's head boiled with caper sauce". Tea in the afternoon might have included fancy cakes. And dinner might have been steak and chips, sweet, cheese and biscuits. Fresh fruit, such as apples and pears, was plentiful.

However, even richer children often ate very simple food. Margaret Steven (b.1911):

There was nothing rich or attractive. All that was downstairs. The food in the nursery was very very plain. Lots of rice

20 A family at tea, 1910.

pudding, lots of stews, porridge always for breakfast (and you had to eat your porridge). For tea there was bread and margarine with jam, but if you wanted bread and butter you weren't allowed to have any jam. And I can remember the stale cake coming up from downstairs. We never got any new cake. And this wasn't a question of money.

Lower-middle-class children
Children in a lower-middle-class family might have started the day with porridge, tea, and toast or bread with either margarine or jam. The main, midday meal might have been boiled mutton and pearl barley as a soup, or a stew or meat pudding. Towards the end of the week the main meal might have been simply cheese. For another such family the cooked breakfast might have been bacon or tripe and onions. The midday meal might have been a chop, vegetables and sweet. Cakes, bread and cheese would have been served at tea. Biscuits and hot milk were served as supper. It was common for servants to eat with the family in lower-middle-class households.

Meals were rather formal occasions for most children in such families. Grace was said, and children were supposed to hold their knives and forks correctly and not to speak. However, there were exceptions to this. In the Shetlands, for example, the meal was served in a big dish set in the middle of the table. Children could join in the conversation and leave the table as they liked.

In a rural area like the Shetlands much of the food was home-grown. Breakfast might have included home-baked bread, and bacon and eggs produced on the croft itself. The main meal at midday might have been mutton from the croft or perhaps fish caught with their own boat, and home-grown vegetables. Tea might have been eggs, bread, oatcakes and home-made rhubarb jam.

Working-class children
Working-class families, in the country and in the towns, fared less well. Here too children were mostly expected to listen and not to talk. The children of one skilled worker would breakfast on porridge, or bread and half an egg (a whole egg on Easter Day only). Bread and jam was usual for tea, with occasional treats. The main midday meal, for which some fathers came home briefly, might have been stew, or a potato pie. If times were hard, a soup was made from a bone from the butcher's and some onions, carrots and cabbage. A rice pudding or a banana chopped in milk might have followed. (Many workers did not come home for the midday meal. Either one of the children took it to them at work, or the men took a sandwich lunch with them.)

The children of one semi-skilled farm labourer were poorly fed for two meals of the day on only tea and bread with jam or lard. A batter or suet pudding might have done for the main meal. Meat could be afforded only once a week. Sunday dinner might have been a soup of meat bones boiled with peas and dumplings. The children of a semi-skilled quarryman did better, with meat about three times a week. Rabbit pie or liver were likely dishes. Bread and jam were home-made and vegetables came from the garden.

Poor families
Poor children were lucky to get meat even at a weekend meal. Cheap cuts sold off by the butcher as stale and stale bread were often all that could be afforded. Broken eggs, broken biscuits, bruised fruit — the market left-overs — were staple fare for the poor. Their basic diet was tea and bread with jam or dripping.

The father usually ate first, in order to keep up his strength for work. Next came any children who were earning. The youngest had simply to hope that there would be enough left for them. Little girls were often

21 1912. East End children waiting for a free dinner at a hall in Salmon's Lane. Many of their fathers were on strike. Employment (and earnings for food) were anyway very insecure. In 1916 still only one third of the workforce was covered by unemployment insurance.

given very little food, as many mothers felt that the lads needed it more. Sunday midday dinner, when the whole family ate together, was often the only reasonable meal many children had all week.

However poor the family, they tried to buy butter when they could. "Maggie Ann" (margarine) was seen as a symbol of poverty. Flo Connors (b.1901) had baked potatoes in their jackets, "one of them and margarine for tea. There was eight of us children and we'd all sit along the table for them."

Poor families made do as they could. A penny-worth of "parings" was a handful of left-overs from a tripe shop, wrapped in newspaper. Another economy meal was "brewis" — some bread and salted dripping broken up in boiling water.

It was estimated in 1904 that at least one third of working-class children were sometimes hungry. Some would wait outside factory gates asking the workers as they came out for any left-overs from their dinners. There were no regular school meals until the Education (Provision of Meals) Act of 1906.

Cooking

Many people still did their cooking on open fires, since gas-rings and gas stoves were only just coming in. Albert Edwards (b. 1904 in Wales):

We used to have a big fire and an oven each side. In the chimney we'd have a bar and a hook coming down, a big pot full of water.

Most food was not sold pre-packed. Albert Edwards:

There wasn't all the tinned stuff what there is now. Everything used to be in a big lump. Before you'd buy cheese, they used to have a round scoop. They'd dig it in and you'd taste the cheese. You never used to buy cheese until you'd tasted it.

For Edith Storry (b.1894) who had no refrigerator,

You just bought food practically as you wanted it. You kept food in a larder, buy enough for each day.

Florence Goddard (b.1892):

We didn't get so much fruit as we get today. Oranges was only at Christmas.

Sweets
Children spent much of their pocket money on sweets. Edith Storry (b.1894):

I liked "cupid favours". An ounce you used to get for a penny. Our halfpenny went a long way. We were about 14 before our pocket money was raised to a penny.

22 1902. Multiple chain stores , such as the Maypole Dairy Co., were first established in the 1870s, and nearly all dealt in food. Edith Storry (b.1894): "They would cut off a pound of butter and put it on the scale. You could go in a small shop, buy a halfpence of jam, a halfpence of sugar, a halfpence of tea. You take a cup along." Children spent much time running errands to shops like this.

Albert Edwards (b.1904 in Wales) bought aniseed balls: "You used to get forty for a penny." Margaret and Pam Steven (b.1911 and 1908) liked the lovely jars of sweets in the shop-window:

> There were no packaged sweets. All were weighed out in brass scales and put in little triangular cones that went in your pocket. The top folded over. You could get an ounce or half an ounce.

Drink

In early Edwardian times children were allowed inside public houses. Rowntree's 1901 survey showed that nearly one quarter of the customers in one pub in York were children getting jugs filled with beer for their parents to drink at home. However, after the Children Act of 1909 no child was allowed into a bar serving alcoholic drinks.

Public houses were open throughout the day and drunkenness was a big problem. With no television or radio, beer drinking was the most common leisure activity. There were still 100,000 public houses in England and Wales in 1908. Many people drank not only for pleasure, but also because getting drunk made them forget the harsh poverty in which they lived. But while getting drunk was a way of escaping from daily life, it still caused further poverty and misery for children in many homes. In some families as much as one third of all earnings went on drink.

Only a few soft drinks existed for Edwardian children. Herb beer was sold in stone bottles. Lemonade and ginger beer were also popular.

Country children like Albert Edwards (b.1904 in Wales) had milk straight from the cow. City children like Dorothy Fyson (b.1909) got their milk from the milkman who came round in a two-wheeled float drawn by a horse. The float contained a large, galvanized milk-churn. The milkman called twice a day:

> You took your milk-jug to the door, and he ladled the milk into it from a large can he carried round. You put a small can outside the door to be filled on the early morning round. We had a very nice milkman who used to give me rides in his float.

23   1912. Pocket money often went on sweets and ice cream. Many children earned their own pocket money by work and other means. Fred Hillsdon (b.1906) scrounged in dustbins to find jam jars which "you could get a halfpenny on if you took it back to the shop".

7 Clothes

24 1908. Looser clothes for girls set the stage for less restricting women's clothes too. For example, the loose hip-line waist worn by girls before the First World War came to dominate adult women's fashion in the 1920s.

Before the nineteenth century children's clothing mainly copied adults' clothing. But this idea gradually changed during the years 1810-1910. While the Edwardian lady had a tightly constricted waistline helped by an S-shaped corset, young girls wore loose frocks with a much more natural line.

Women's clothes generally began to appear trimmer in the 1900s. The bell-shaped skirt and high-necked blouse of late Victorian times were worn until 1908, when the narrower hobble skirt became fashionable. Clothes then began to follow the natural female figure more. A more youthful style came in. The brassière was introduced in about 1913, part of the Edwardian era's idea of more comfortable underclothes for women.

Girls' underwear

Girls at this time were wearing the liberty bodice, which was introduced in 1908 and which lasted as underwear until the 1950s. It was a soft, front-buttoning bodice made of finely knitted cotton stockinette in a natural colour. Bands of tape kept it in place. Suspenders were fitted to the hem to hold up stockings. Already at the turn of the century the term "drawers" was less used and the words "knickers" or "bloomers" were replacing it.

Dorothy Fyson (b.1909) wore masses of underclothes. "Combinations" were close-fitting, rather like a leotard, with a gap at the bottom:

25 Liberal supporters in a bye-election, 1913. Clothes clearly distinguished the classes in Edwardian times. There were those with tailor-made clothes, those who wore the new ready-mades, and the poor who could only afford well-worn cast-offs.

We always wore white knickers with frills and always two petticoats, a flannel or flannelette one and a white cotton frilly one on top. My mother thought herself very modern when she dressed me in navy-blue bloomers to match my navy serge school dress my first winter at school (1914).

Girls' dresses

The starched white "pinny" or pinafore was the main girls' dress at the start of the Edwardian era. This was originally a bib-apron. By 1910 the pinny was no longer as popular, being somewhat replaced by simpler dresses like the gym slip. But Cedric Fyson's (b.1903) older sisters wore pinafores up until about the First World War. And Dorothy Fyson (b.1909) always wore one as a small child:

They were often very fancy affairs, with a flounce at the bottom usually edged with broderie anglaise, and similar flounces on the shoulders.

The freer clothing for girls in the 1900s was largely the result of changes in girls' schooling in the late nineteenth century. As games and gymnastics were introduced into the syllabus, looser clothing was needed. The gym slip gradually became the school uniform in many cases. Most school uniforms began as sports clothes, in the case of boys as well as girls.

Girls' footwear

Outdoor footwear for girls were low-heeled boots up to the ankle or up to the calf. Small buttons fastened these. Some had elastic panels on the sides. Patent-leather pumps sometimes had fancy buckles. Indoor slippers were often decorated with embroidery or beadwork. Clogs were standard footwear for girls working in mills. (Shawls were similarly a typical item of mill-girls' clothing.)

Boys' clothes

It was not until Edwardian times that most small boys were dressed in trousers. Before 1901 many boys as well as girls had been in skirts until the age of about four. However, in Edwardian times knickerbockers (usually called just knickers) were common boys' wear. According to Cedric Fyson (b.1903), young boys often still wore

their knickers to just below the knee, where they were fastened by one or two buttons. My mother did not like these,

so I continued to wear shorts until I went into long trousers at the age of about fourteen or fifteen — very much later than boys would tolerate now!

Rubber garters were often worn to hold up stockings. Celluloid collars were worn by many boys, except the poorest.

Walking-shoes began to replace ankle-boots for boys by the early 1900s, but ankle-boots were still worn (especially by poorer boys) well into Edwardian times. Clogs were also worn for everyday.

Clothes for men and boys were still in the sombre colours worn by men since the mid-nineteenth century. Some men continued to wear top hats and frock-coats right up to the First World War.

26 1912. A father holding pawn tickets. It was often the family's Sunday clothes (boots, suits, clean dresses) that were pawned to raise money. Pledging time was usually Monday and the goods were collected on Saturday. Interest of one penny in the shilling had to be paid on what had been borrowed.

Poor and working-class children

The poorest children went barefoot in summer and depended on the police and charities to find them boots for going to school. Clothes were bought second-hand at markets and cheap sales. An average working-class family was able to buy some new clothes and shoes (mainly for Sunday wear), but everyday clothes were often second-hand.

Hats

Men and women — except for the very poor — all wore hats in the street. Children too often wore caps or hats.

Knitting

Many children had their clothes hand-made. In Shetland clothes were knitted

28   1902. Elaborate hats, fur-trimmed coats and muffs were all part of the fancy dressing of children early in the century. Heavily starched cotton dresses were often embroidered and lace-trimmed for best. All this ended during the First World War, when simpler fashions (which had been gradually taking over) were the rule.

from the wool of the family's own sheep. The wool was carded and spun all at home, with children helping.

Best clothes

There were, of course, all sorts of outfits in which well-off children were dressed for best. The "Buster Brown" suit for small boys became popular in about 1908, based on an American comic-strip character. The Eton suit, with top hat and stiffly starched collar, was worn by the public school boys on their 4 June boat event day. It became a fashion for Sunday best copied for other boys as well.

Meanwhile, the poorest children made do with what could be found for them. Often they had layers of odd clothes piled on for warmth. Such children were glad to have two shoes that matched, "near enough".

27   1902. A popular novelty costume for boys was the sailor-suit.

8 Work

The first job that I did was in the tobacconist. We used to open the shop at six o'clock in the morning and close it at eleven o'clock at night. I was there the whole time, six days a week.

Edith Storry was 14 when she started work at the tobacconist's in 1908.

Poor working conditions were common in the early 1900s. Under 20 per cent of employees were organized in unions and even those had little power. The working week was generally longer than it is now — usually 54 hours, starting at 6.00 a.m. and finishing at 5.30 p.m.

Child workers

Even younger Edwardian children than Edith Storry did all sorts of odd jobs to earn money. They went out running errands, washing steps and window-sills, delivering

29 1907. A flower girl sells buttonholes to Eton boys who are dressed for their 4 June boat day celebrations. Children watched and took part in the many street industries of the day. There were the china-menders, chair-menders, woolwork-picture-makers, net-makers. Besides greengrocers and shoeblacks, there were sellers of old hats, fish, crumpets, watercress, windmills and so on. The toffee man could be watched making his product on the spot.

30 1910. A mine near Cardiff. According to the 1911 Census report for Britain, about 10 per cent of employed males under the age of eighteen worked in or around mines. The Coal Mines Act of 1911 made it illegal for boys under 14 to work below ground.

meat or milk, selling papers or matches in the street, and carrying bags. The money children earned in this way was often handed over to the parents as an important part of the family's income. The Census report for 1911 showed that about one in six children aged 10-13 were in some kind of paid employment.

Lulu Lee, aged 12 in 1901, went step-cleaning:

> I used to go to all the different houses, tupence and thrupence. One house used to give me a jar of jam for me mum every Saturday. I used to go out in the morning, just after nine and stay out nearly all day. Take your apron and a bag for your money.

Some schoolchildren as young as eight were found to be working more than 19 hours a week. One report told of a 12 year-old boy who rose two mornings a week at 2.30 a.m., the other five at 4.30 a.m. for a three-mile walk to a water-cress bed. He washed and sold cresses every available hour when he was not at school.

There were laws protecting children. Since the first Factory Act of 1802 there had been increasing control and inspection of how children were worked by their employers. But a Committee set up in 1901 to report to the Home Office estimated that some 300,000 children were still combining school attendance with paid employment. The report was not against the idea of children doing some work ("moderate work under healthy conditions may be and in most cases will be a benefit.") But it was concerned for the over 50,000 children who were being worked more than 20 hours a week on top of the 27½ hours a week spent at school.

34

One case mentioned by the Committee was that of an 11 year-old boy who, for four shillings a week, worked 43¾ hours carrying parcels from a chemist's shop. Except on Sundays, practically every moment of his life was spent at school or at work, from seven o'clock in the morning until nine o'clock at night.

A series of Education Acts beginning in 1870 had made it illegal to regularly employ children except by means of the half-time system or out of school hours. Therefore by 1901 the employment of children in most large industries was carefully controlled and children were not allowed to work during school hours. But, as the 1901 Committee report said:

Their employment in other occupations outside school hours is wholly unregulated . . . . Provided they make eight or ten school attendances every week they may be employed in the streets, in the fields, in shops or at home for the longest possible hours and on the hardest and most irksome work, without any limit or regulation.

Under the "half-time" system, children aged 12 and over (with very basic skills learnt at school) could work in factories either in the morning or in the afternoon, or on alternate days. Half-time attendance at school was required. Most half-timers worked in the cotton-spinning mills and weaving sheds of Lancashire or in the woollen and worsted factories of Yorkshire. Some also worked in farming. There were still over 80,000 half-timers in 1907 and the system did not fade until 1918.

Full-time work in factories and workshops was allowed for children over 13 who had certain skills from school. The longest children were allowed to work in home factories and workshops was 39 hours a week, excluding mealtimes. In mines, boys over the age of 13 were allowed to work underground. (This age limit was raised to 14 in 1911.)

31 A Lancashire cotton mill in the early 1900s. Many children as young as 12 were "half-timers" in such factories. Work began at 6.00 a.m. Half-timers worked for six hours, with a half-hour stop for breakfast at 8 o'clock. Then they went to dinner and spent the afternoon at school. The atmosphere in mills like this was hot, damp and noisy, and the machinery was very dangerous. The younger the children employed, the higher the rate of accidents. The industrial death rate was five times higher then than in the 1970s.

Shops

By 1901 most children in employment worked in or for shops. Some 100,000 were so employed, with at least 40,000 of these working for newsagents. The morning delivery of milk was another common job for children. Often the work began at 5.00 or 5.30 a.m., and so some three hours could be worked before school. Lather boys in barber's shops worked the longest hours and often in bad sanitary conditions. Many witnesses for the 1901 report "named this as the one employment for boys which they would wish to see totally prohibited". Lather boys often worked five hours every evening, fifteen hours on Saturday and six or eight hours on Sunday.

Domestic work

Many children — about 50,000 in 1901 — earned money by domestic work. A number of boys found early morning jobs for an hour or two cleaning knives and boots and carrying coals. Many girls were employed as baby-minders and housemaids.

Outdoor work

Work in agriculture occupied some 40-50,000 children in 1901. Farm work was thought healthy by virtue of the fresh country air. More worry was felt for city children hawking and selling on the streets. There were some 25,000 of these. The 1901 report said of the street sellers:

This work is carried on by a worse class of children and under worse moral influences than any other.

A Miss Macleod reporting to a Scottish Committee told how on one evening in 1908 she

visited six Model Lodging Houses where many of the young street-traders sleep. We saw scores of children — many of them quite young. These children pay

32 1908. Employment was more individual and ► personal in Edwardian times. Assistants were taken on by local craftsmen and shopowners, and labourers by local manufacturers and builders. Family firms were still very common. About one eighth of the workforce were either employers or self-employed (twice the proportions of the 1970s).

3d a night for their bed and are admitted at any hour of the night.

It was mainly older boys who slept in the "Models" but Miss Macleod found that "three of the street sellers were only eight years old, three were under 10, two under 12, and two were 13."

Children did all kinds of other work. One common job was to rouse early workers by tapping with a long cane on bedroom windows. Of course, this job meant the children had to be up at a very early hour themselves, and it was often combined with other work such as delivering milk.

Edwardian improvements for child workers

The 1901 report suggested that bye-laws should be made by County and Borough Councils to further control conditions and hours of work by children. More reports and laws during Edwardian times gradually did restrict child employment. For example, the Employment of Children Act 1903 included such points as that

a child [under 14] shall not be employed between the hours of nine in the evening and six in the morning . . . [and] . . . a child under the age of eleven years shall not be employed in street trading.

However, in 1914 *The Women's Industrial News* complained that not enough bye-

33 Norfolk turkey farm, 1908. Many children ► under 12 combined school with helping on a farm. This often meant doing hours of work in the morning before school started.

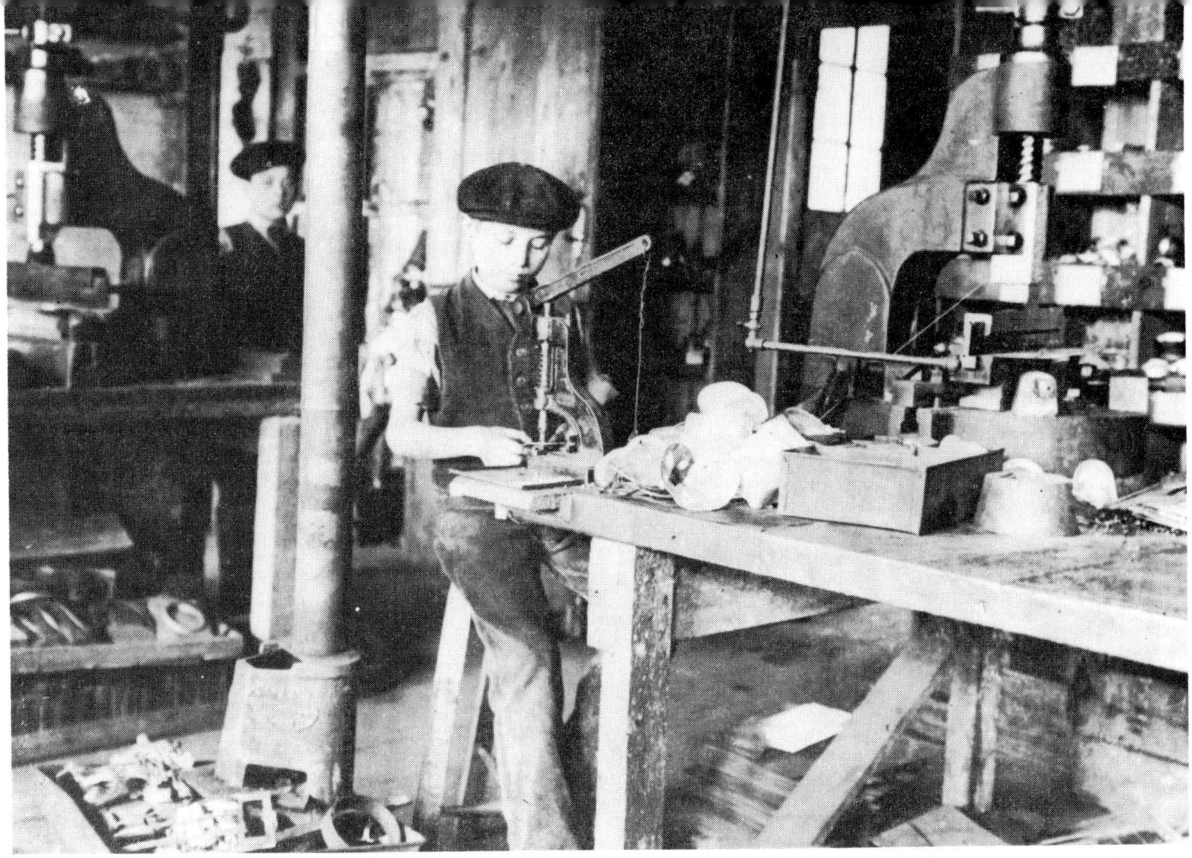

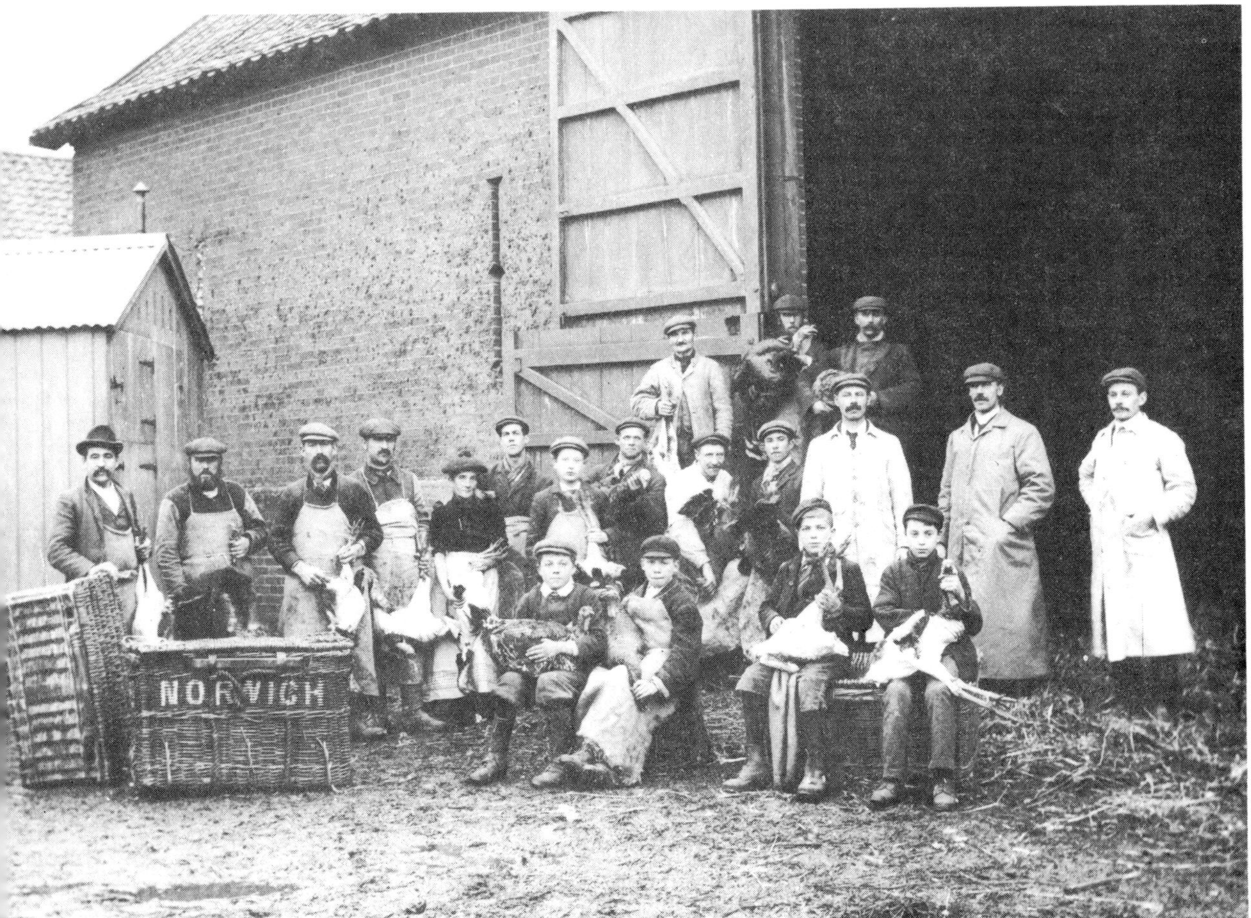
NORVICH

laws were being passed, and that even where laws existed they were not being enforced.

By 1910 the statistics of the Liverpool Education Office showed that of some 37,000 children in state schools between the ages of 11 and 14, about one in seven was also a wage-earner. Some 500 of these children worked for over 18 hours a week in addition to spending some 30 hours a week in school.

Concern was growing that working school-children were often too sleepy in school to benefit much from their lessons. There was also concern for their health. A doctor's report on the health of some 384 wage-earning schoolboys was that

233 showed signs of fatigue
140 were anaemic
131 had severe nerve signs
 64 suffered from deformities resulting from the carrying of heavy weights
 51 had severe heart signs

34 "Hoppers" arriving at the Kentish hop-fields, 1910. The hop-growing counties were easily reached from London. Each year East Enders went to pick the hops and so had a short break from city life.

A Devon County Council report of 1913 quoted several teachers on the problem. One headmaster of a village school with 91 children said that about 10 of these were in difficulty because of outside work:

I have the case of a boy. As a rule, he has to milk six cows in the morning before starting for school, and he has to clean out very often many of the stalls, and the poor little chap — he is twelve years old — when he comes to school he very often lies down and goes to sleep. He has been seen by some of the managers running as hard as he could to school to save his attendance mark. Since last Easter up to today he has been late 65 times.

Another headmaster quoted in the report said:

Within the past two years four different boys have had this job. The boy has to walk 3½ miles out to the railway station to fetch the *Morning News* — anything from twenty to fifty papers. That means seven miles. He starts at 6.30 in the

morning, gets out there and back, delivers some papers and gets to school at nine o'clock. Frequently if it is a wet morning he gets wet through and I have to send him to my own house to dry by the kitchen fire. In the winter, of course, we have the stove in the school . . . . It is too much for them . . . . A boy may be a very good scholar before he starts as an errand boy. When he goes carrying heavy baskets of groceries, meat and bread there is always a deterioration in his work after that.

School-leavers

As well as worry about schoolchildren at work, there was growing concern about what children did when they left school. A 1910 report by the Poor Law Commissioners noted that some 70-80 per cent of boys entered unskilled jobs on leaving school. Many of these were blind-alley jobs leading nowhere:

At 17 or 18 the crisis comes. The employer who wants a boy at boys' wages sends him away at a week's notice and starts again with a new boy fresh from school.

A survey of nearly one thousand boys and one thousand girls leaving school in June 1910 showed that 71 per cent of the boys became errand boys or took on other casual jobs. Only about 300 went into offices or other jobs likely to lead to more permanent employment. Of the girls, less than one third went into jobs. Of these, 113 went into dressmaking, tailoring and millinery, 14 went into offices, 41 into factories and workshops, 39 became shop assistants, 7 laundresses, 81 domestic servants and 7 did other jobs. A 1907 survey showed that

half the girls between 13 and 18 are still engaged washing, cleaning, cooking and mending within the four walls of their own or someone else's home.

35 A messenger boy, 1907. To work as a messenger or van boy was very common. The 1911 Census for Britain showed that more than 5 per cent of 13 year-olds were so employed, more than 16 per cent of 14 year-olds, and more than 13 per cent of 15 year-olds.

Domestic service

Florence Goddard (b.1892), like very many girls, went into service at the age of 13. It was up at six in the morning, work until late in the evening. The family had dinner at about eight o'clock, and all the washing-up had to be done before she could be in bed, at about ten o'clock. Part of her job was to make the early morning fires and to have boiling water ready for when the barber came to shave the master. Her room at the top of the house had no heating:

I remember waking up to find ice in the basin. You had to break the ice before you could wash.

Florence and other young servants had one afternoon off a week, plus every other Sunday. One of her least favourite jobs was having to pluck and clean freshly killed chickens.

36 1905. Domestic servants (housemaids, cooks, gardeners, etc) were a large part of the Edwardian workforce. The percentage of workers in service was still 14 per cent in 1911 — more than 2½ million people, compared to just over 100,000 in the 1970s. Young people often started full-time as a domestic servant at the age of 13. The numbers began to fall in late Edwardian times as new jobs opened up in clerical work, shop work, and the public services.

9 Education

Early twentieth-century reforms known together as the "children's charter" included the setting up of the Board of Education in 1900. An Education Act of 1902 then laid the basis for the modern state educational system in Britain.

In 1870 School Boards had been established in areas where there were not enough voluntary schools. The job of the Boards was to set up new schools to fill the gaps. A local rate was raised to help pay for the new Board Schools. Schooling had been made compulsory to age 10 by 1880, and compulsory to age 12 by 1899.

37 1906. Mass drill at a state elementary school. Emphasis was laid on physical training, partly because so many young men had been rejected as unfit for service in the Second Boer War (1899-1902).

The 1902 Education Act ended the School Boards and turned the counties and county boroughs into education authorities. For the first time elementary and higher education were jointly controlled by the new education authorities, although a clear distinction was made between elementary and secondary schools. Secondary schools included the independent public and grammar schools and the new local authority day grammar schools (mainly fee-paying, for children from the age of seven or eight).

Most children attended only the free elementary schools and left at the age of twelve. Fewer than 20 per cent of Edwardian boys attended any kind of secondary school. Most who did were middle class. Under 10 per cent of working-class boys continued at school after the elementary stage — and only about one per cent of those were from the families of semi-skilled or unskilled manual workers.

The school-leaving age was not raised from 12 to 14 until 1918. But spending on education did increase markedly in Edwardian times. The average number of children to one teacher in each elementary school class was about 50. (In poorer areas there were often 60 children per teacher.) In secondary schools there were about 17 pupils in each class.

State secondary schools

1904 regulations for state secondary schools steered them towards providing the same kind of education as was offered by the independent schools:

> The course should provide for instruction in the English Language and Literature, at least one Language other than English, Geography, History, Mathematics, Science and Drawing, with due provision for Manual Work and Physical Exercises, and in a girls' school, for Housewifery.

The secondary schools were mostly single-sex.

In 1907 all secondary schools receiving some public money were required to have

38 Schoolboys on strike in Shoreditch, London in 1911. There were many workers' strikes in 1911 and 1912. Schoolchildren joined the general unrest by having school walk-outs. They asked for no more caning — and in some places strikers also demanded pocket money in return for going to school.

39 A drawing class at a state elementary school in the early 1900s. Drawing was encouraged, but the idea was to draw an object "as it is". There was little idea of creative expression. Note the iron-framed desks which were bolted to the stepped floor. Children were not able to move about freely.

free places for 25 per cent of all the children entering each year. "11 plus" was set up as the age when elementary school pupils would sit an exam to try to qualify for a free place. The new "free-placers" came mainly from the lower middle class.

Punishments and rewards

In many Edwardian schools pupils were caned if they failed to know the answers, or if they talked out of turn — sometimes even if they just coughed. Teachers were known to pull hair and throw books. Discipline could be harsh. For example, Edith Storry (b.1894) was hit on the knuckles for being left-handed.

There were prizes for doing well. At Florence Goddard's (b.1892) school there were prizes for subjects like knitting, arithmetic and geography. Flo Connors (b.1901) had needlework twice a week and they "used to get a prize if it was the best".

Nursery school

Education at this time could boast that nearly 50 per cent of children aged three and four were in nursery school. These young classes were quite modern in their activities — dancing, games, handwork, singing. The freer approach spread only very slowly to older children. A number of private progressive schools did start in Edwardian years.

Elementary school

At the age of five children went into what was called "Standard I", then "Standard II", etc. There were simple expectations of what a child should be able to do before he could pass from one Standard to the next.

Albert Edwards (b. 1904 in Wales):

When we went to school we always had to have a starched collar on, nice and stiff and clean, and you had to have your shoes clean. When you went into class you had to pull up your sleeve and teacher would look to see if your wrist was clean, and the back of your neck. If you hadn't washed the back of your neck you were sent out and it was given a scrub.

Schooling for the upper classes

In the public schools the emphasis was on Classics and games. Some richer children received education at home from governesses and tutors. Besides learning literature, art and languages, they might also have had a music teacher who taught them violin and piano.

Education after school

Only the very few went to university, although the universities did expand during Edward's reign. But Britain still had many fewer students in higher education than Germany, France and America.

The 1902 Education Act also led to the expansion of teacher-training colleges and the dying out of what was called "the pupil-teacher system". In 1902 55 per cent of teachers had not been to a training college of any kind. Since 1846 the system had been for older elementary school pupils wanting to become teachers to apprentice themselves for a five-year period to a head teacher. During this time they helped to teach classes and were themselves taught outside school hours by the head. By the late nineteenth century pupil-teacher centres or "colleges" had been set up to back up the instruction given by heads. But, from 1902, future teachers were expected to go on from elementary school to secondary school and then to a proper training college.

Private colleges began after 1900 to teach typing, bookkeeping, shorthand and other technical and commercial skills. There was a growing demand for these skills but as yet little education available from the state.

Sunday school

Many children were sent to Sunday school. Some, like Fred Hillsdon (b.1906), never got there:

Five boys in my family, five of us. Sunday school meant going there and reading all these prayers and that. We didn't fancy that so we used to go to the museums instead. But then once a year there was what they called a Sunday school treat. One of the big gardens used to be open for the children and the vicar would give out tea and buns, balloons and everything like that. Well, of course, us poor little lot we hadn't got a ticket. Our mother rushes round saying "Why hasn't my boys got a ticket?" He said "When your boys come to Sunday school they'll get a ticket."

40   1912. Pupils of Miss Morris, a London actress-manageress, learn to dance. Dancing lessons and music lessons were popular out-of-school education.

10 Books and Newspapers

41   1909. Arthur Rackham was a popular illustrator of children's books, such as *Grimms' Fairy Tales* **(1900),** *Rip Van Winkle* **(1905) and** *Gulliver's Travels* **(1909).**

A number of famous children's books date from Edwardian times and just before. Beatrix Potter's *Peter Rabbit* appeared in 1900, J.M. Barrie's *Peter Pan* in 1904, and

Kenneth Grahame's *The Wind in the Willows* in 1908. Rag-books too began in the early 1900s.

In addition to books there were periodicals. The Victorian "penny dreadful" was changed in the 1890s to a weekly paper with serial adventure and school stories. These "Old Boy's Books" as they are now known began with a paper called *Chum* in 1892. By 1914 there were many more, such as *The Gem*, *Union Jack*, and *The Magnet*. They had spy stories and detective stories in them. Characters from these were then sometimes featured in regular periodicals of their own. *Greyfriars* was devoted to tales of the very popular Frank Richards' character Billy Bunter and his schoolfriends. The detective serial *Sexton Blake* was another great favourite.

There were no books at all in many lower-working-class households. It was thought in many homes that books kept children from getting on with useful tasks. Some homes had only the books which had been presented to the children for regular attendance at Sunday school. These were often treated as decorations, certainly not to be handled by children. Margaret Steven (b.1911):

> We were given beautiful books. They were kept downstairs and on Sundays when we went downstairs our father used to read to us.

Libraries

Public libraries had begun in the mid-nineteenth century, but it was 1906 before children under 14 were allowed to belong to them. Children of 10 and over were then allowed to take out one book a fortnight. Library stocks doubled between 1901 and 1914 but many people still could not even read.

Newspapers

Popular newspapers began in the late nineteenth and early twentieth centuries. By 1908 there were over twenty national morning papers and nine evening papers. But daily papers were still read by about one fifth of adults only. Many more saw only the Sunday papers. Newspapers generally were thought not proper for children and were kept from them.

11 Toys and Games

New toys

Teddy bears were born in 1903. The idea came from a newspaper photograph of the US President Teddy Roosevelt in the Rocky Mountains with a small brown bear at his feet. The founder of the American Ideal Toy Corporation wrote to Roosevelt asking if he could produce a small toy bear and call it "Teddy's Bear". The toy spread quickly to many other countries, including Britain.

Another toy still popular today which began in Edwardian times is Meccano. It was first patented in 1901 and its early name was "Mechanics Made Easy". The name was changed to Meccano in 1907. Model aeroplanes were also new at this time. One of the earliest appeared in 1904. Child-size motor cars were first produced in about 1905.

Hollow moulded rubber dolls date from the turn of the century too. These were immediately popular as bath toys. Squeaking devices were added to them in the early twentieth century. Pocket-sized puzzles also date from the early 1900s. These were in metal with polished wood pieces that slid up and down or across.

Old toys

Many toys and games carried on from Victorian times and earlier — board-games, like chess, chequers, for example. The range of model shops expanded greatly in Edwardian days to include banks, railway booking offices, post offices (complete with toy stamps and stationery). Tin-plate toys which had appeared in late Victorian times were also popular. The toys were stamped out of tin-plate, crudely assembled and then painted. An example from 1910 was a delivery van, complete with driver and sacks and painted advertisements. Miniature kitchen stoves and cookers in tin-plate, with sets of pots and pans to match, were much in demand. Cast-metal

42 1906. The two older girls hold dolls, while the small girl shares her seat with an early teddy bear.

models of motor-cars, locomotives, aircraft and ships began to replace tin-plate ones in the 1900s because they could be far more accurate.

Train sets were great favourites from the Victorian era on. The richer Edwardian child might have had a steam locomotive with a tiny boiler fired by a spirit lamp. But the mass of children had only clockwork train sets. Clockwork wind-up toys of all kinds were very popular. Electrically driven toys had existed already at the end of the nineteenth century, but were very expensive and not much seen until the 1920s. A wooden truck powered by a battery motor was only for the few in 1905. Assembly toys were also expensive then.

Toy soldiers were another favourite Edwardian toy. In 1905 some five million of these existed in over one hundred varieties.

Educational toys

The "Educational Board" was a board with indentations in the shape of wooden silhouettes of simple objects. The "top hat" was one familiar shape which young children had to fit into the right hole.

Dolls

Dolls have always been popular. The years 1900-1910 were the day of the mechanical novelty doll. Already in the late nineteenth century there had been talking dolls, dolls taking liquid from feeding bottles, and so on. Before the First World War toy departments in large department stores sold vast ranges of accessories such as hats and shoes to fit all sizes of dolls.

Papier-mâché finished with a coating of wax was used for dolls' heads. More expensive dolls were made of porcelain. Most rag-dolls were home-made, but in 1908 it was possible to buy sheets of calico on which were printed the outline of a doll's body and face — a sort of rag-doll kit. The golliwog with its black face, pop eyes and big, red mouth was first a character in a book in 1895 and was then made as a doll by toymakers.

Doll's houses were less carefully made than in earlier times. From about 1904 they were often of pasteboard and hardboard with painted brickwork and roof-tiles. There were special prams for dolls which in 1908 had names like "The Lady" and "The Elegance".

Hoops

Hoops were still popular. Cedric Fyson (b.1903):

Girls and small boys had wooden hoops, which they struck with a hoop-stick. I well remember my feeling of superiority when, as an older boy (probably aged about ten), I was given an iron hoop. This was propelled by a "skimmer", an iron hook with a wooden handle.

According to Albert Edwards (b.1904), hoops were called "bowles" in Wales.

You'd think nothing of running miles with them. There was plenty of blacksmiths around in them days. When a bowle would break, you'd just go in there, give him a hapenny and he'd join it together again.

Home-made toys were all that many children had. As a tiny boy in Ireland, Edmund Dalton (b.1909) "kicked a rag ball around. We couldn't afford to buy a leather one so we used to make one of rags tied together."

Street games

Many street games were played by Edwardian children. "Tip-cat" started in the country and soon spread to every town. The tip-cat was simply a piece of wood tapered to a point at each end. It was hit on one end, which made it shoot up in the air. Then

43 1904. Pull-along toys were favourites of ► younger children. There were pull-along buses, trains, and even such a typically Edwardian item as a water wagon which sprinkled the streets to keep down the dust. Most common of all were the barrel-shaped, beech-wood horses like the one in the photo. Rocking-horses too were popular in the nursery.

you hit it again with a stick, sending it whizzing away. While very popular with children, the pastime was far from pleasing to the owners of broken windows! The police tried in vain to stop it.

Another rough game especially liked by children in slum areas was "Jimmy-Jimmy-Knacker" (also called "Strong Horse"). The boys divided themselves into two sides. The leader of one team stood with his face to a wall, and his team lined up closely behind him, one behind the other, each bending over with arms around the boy in front's waist. This team was the "horse". One after another the boys of the other team then jumped on the bent backs, banging them as hard as they could. The boys below tried to dump their "riders". Finally something gave way: either the "horse" broke down or the riders were

thrown and the game would start again.

In "Ugly Bear" one boy crawled along the pavement and the other boys tried to hit him with caps attached to lengths of string. "Tom-Tiddlers-Ground" was played over the entire length of a street. The players formed long lines on either side while a keeper guarded the centre of the road. The aim was to cross the street without being caught. Anyone caught "trespassing" on the centre could be taken captive. Children galloped wildly up the sides of the street in search of an unguarded spot to cross.

44 1908. Hoops were a favourite toy for rich and poor. Margaret Steven (b.1911): "Children would put the hoop over their hips and waggle them. Also we used to skip into them. And you could roll them along."

Songs

Songs and chants used for counting and skipping were as popular then as they have been throughout the ages. One rhyme of 1910 went:

> *Far are ye gaein'?*
> *Across the gutter.*
> *Fat for?*
> *A pund o'butter.*
> *Far's yer money?*
> *In my pocket.*
> *Far's ye pocket?*
> *Clean forgot it!*

Iona and Peter Opie included this in a book first published in 1959 called *The Lore and Language of Schoolchildren*. They showed how close it was to a Mother Goose rhyme of 1780 and also to a chant used for counting in 1950. The songs and games of children have changed really very little over the centuries.

Games with small objects

Edwardian children made great use of everyday buttons in their games. Every button had a special value. There were three main types — "sinkeys", "shankeys" and "liveries". Sinkeys were metal buttons with a hollow centre, shankeys were large buttons attached by wire, and liveries were buttons with crests (very much prized).

In one favourite button game the buttons were thrown against a wall so that they would bounce towards a line or a hole in the ground. A "knicker" (small, circular metal piece) was often used to drive buttons one way or another. The goal of all the games, of course, was to claim the buttons which you hit or put into the hole. For many poor children, a collection of buttons was treasure.

Edwardian children were keen on marbles, "Ring taw" being most popular. A ring was

45   1908. Children made many of their own toys from scraps and whatever they could find.

drawn and each player placed a certain number of marbles inside it. An outer ring known as an offing or bar or taw line was made. From this outer ring players picked off marbles with great skill and concentration.

"Three Holes" or "Duck" was usually played with stones. Three holes were made in the ground and a coat or something similar put in front of each. The aim was to throw stones over the obstacles into the three holes one after the other — if possible hitting a neighbour's stone out.

Girls played a game with four stones which they threw on the pavement, as close together as possible, and a marble held in the right hand. The object was to throw the marble in the air, pick up one of the stones, and catch the marble as it came down. The marble was then thrown again and a second stone picked up, etc. The stones were placed in various ways and had to be handled in special ways between the falls of the marble. The last part was known as the "pegsy": the stones were laid out in a line, the marble thrown, and the first stone had to be picked up and replaced exactly in time for the marble to be caught.

Girls' games
Hopscotch was the great favourite among the girls. On the pavement they marked out various numbered squares, known as "sie". The aim was then to "toe a chip" — a stone, button, or bit of china — into each square in turn. Then the chip was placed on the toe and the player had to hop with it into each of the numbered squares.

Skipping over ropes was another girls' favourite. Flo Connors (b.1901):

You used to skip like hell, wore all our boots out.

Cigarette cards
A game of chance was played with the cardboard pictures that came with packs of cigarettes. Children begged these off men as they came out of tobacconists. A chalk line was made on the pavement and the boys took turns to throw the picture cards towards the line. The boy whose card landed nearest the line had the privilege of picking up the cards and tossing them into the air. All that came down with the picture showing became his.

The cigarette pictures came in series. Albert Edwards (b.1904 in Wales):

They might be about battleships or butterflies. All different subjects like that.

He used to get cards by going down to the railway siding.

As they opened the doors and swept out there used to be hundreds of cards on the side of the track.

Other games
Another game Albert Edwards used to play was "Dickie show your light".

In the winter time we used to get a jam jar, get some boiling water, give the jar a tap and the bottom would come out clean as a whistle. Take a top off a blacking tin, shoe polish tin, put a candle in it and put the jar over that. We were all over the place trying to find one another.

Many other games filled the countryside and streets of Edwardian Britain. Packaback wrestling, street cricket and football, leapfrog, rounders, snowballing, Ring o' Roses, make-believe horses and trains and "mothers and fathers" — the list goes on and on. And after a heavy rain, there were certain to be boys floating paper boats in the gutter.

For a boy sent on an errand, there was always "Kicking the can" to help him resist running off to join his friends. Another favourite errand boy's game was played with a piece of leather attached to a string. The leather was thoroughly soaked in water, so that when it was pressed to a pavement, it stuck tightly. A good pull on the string to unstick it produced a gurgling, sucking sound. This noise-making was, and probably always will be, the delight of small boys.

46 1908. City children made their own swing. They fastened a rope to the bar of a lamppost. Sitting inside the loop, a child wound the rope round the post. As the rope unwound the child would swing in a circle.

12 Mischief, Crime and Punishment

We used to tie people's knockers up, tie knockers from one house to the next. We knocked the knocker and as they came out they knocked the next people.

Fred Hillsdon played many such pranks at the ripe age of seven in 1913. Common tricks included knocking doors ("Knock down ginger") and tapping on a window with a needle tied to a piece of cotton.

It was of course a fine line between common childhood pranks, such as stealing apples from orchards, and what was called crime. Albert Edwards (b. 1904 in Wales):

Outside the shops in them days they used to have pigs hanging, trotters hanging down. We had a sharp knife and we cut a trotter down. They caught us. The policeman threatened to take us down and give us the birch. There was a lot of that in them days. When we got to school, they give us about six hits on each hand till

47 1910. Barefoot slum children look wistfully in a shop window. The poorest children relied on police and charities for clothes, and on free mission suppers and school meals for food. Begging and sleeping out were common "crimes" of the poor which were a result of their rough living conditions.

you could hardly move. Then you go home and tell your mother about it and she gives you another lot. It didn't do us any harm. We was disciplined. We had the old village policeman. When we see him coming along, whether we was doing wrong or not, we'd scoot. Policemen scared the life out of us.

Criminal offences

Theft and vandalism were the main charges against Edwardian youth brought before the courts. But about one third of young people arrested were prosecuted for some street offence such as obstruction. Fining was the usual punishment, but some offenders were sent to an industrial school, whipped, or put on probation. Many thousands of children did go to prison for offences such as not being able to pay a fine, trespassing, throwing snowballs, sleeping out, gambling. Their sentences were usually quite short, three days to one month.

Begging was another crime. As boys, Fred Hillsdon (b.1906) and his friends set up what they called "The Grotto".

We used to get some bits of grass, line it up on the pavement, into a little square, put all sorts of little trinkets in there. Then we used to run after people shouting "please remember the grotto". People gave you a halfpenny, penny, something like that. What the meaning was I'll never know. Course with the grotto you could start up anytime of the year.

Edwardian law reforms for young people

The Youthful Offenders Act of 1901 tried, among other things, to reduce the number of sentences on juveniles under sixteen. In 1905 key reforms asked for were: (1) no more prison for young persons under sixteen; (2) Children's Courts with a selected magistrate; (3) separate places of detention for young persons; (4) Probation Officers to deal with cases of children released under

suspended sentences.

By 1909 these reforms were in effect, as a result of the new Children Act. A 1908 report showed that already some 208 institutions had been dealing with "wayward" children. They included reformatory schools, industrial schools, truant schools, day industrial schools and special homes.

Stealing

As late as in 1833 a boy of nine had been sentenced to hang for stealing paint (he was reprieved). Edwardian Britain was well beyond this, but even so, in 1914, at the tender age of eight, Fred Hillsdon was dragged before a court by two detectives and was sent for a week's remand in a home. His crime? Looking back, Frances, his wife, explained:

In those days we had coal fires but you couldn't afford coal. There were what they used to call tar blocks — wooden blocks in the road sprayed with tar. When the workmen found a place that had to be repaired they used to dig these tar blocks up. We used to go round and pick these blocks up and take them home and put those on the fire. There was lots of children with sacks collecting them.

Fred added:

You were allowed to take the small pieces, the broken ones which they couldn't lay down again. But me, I took the whole ones, a consequence of which I was arrested.

Cars

There were other charges less likely to be made today. In 1908 in Glasgow some 506 boys were in trouble for "swinging on cars" — a crime hardly possible with modern styles.

13 Sport, Entertainment and Holidays

Sport — played and watched

The Edwardian rich devoted much of their time to sporting pursuits. The poor were mainly keen on football. Cricket was less popular among the working classes, but even street urchins were found using dustbins as wickets. Rugby League was considered rather "common", and Rugby Union more for "gents". Middle-class grammar schools were careful to see that pupils played rugby rather than soccer. Hockey was played at universities and the public schools, by females as well as males. Lawn tennis and croquet were generally popular, as were fishing and bicycling.

48 1907. Horse-riding was popular. ►

49 1912. A bicycle is used to tow skaters. Bicycling became popular in the late nineteenth century, and was a great Edwardian pastime. The safety bicycle with even-sized wheels replaced the Victorian penny-farthing (with one large and one small wheel).

▼

Football was far and away the leading spectator sport. As a boy, Fred Hillsdon (b.1906) went to great lengths to see a game:

We couldn't afford to go and see a football match so we found a way of clambering over the wall. We used to climb over and get on the railway track, run along the railway track and climb over the back wall into the grounds. One touch of those live wires . . .

Cinema and theatre

For other entertainments as well, it was largely a matter of "bunking in", for very poor children — going round the back and finding a way in. Fred Hillsdon (b.1906) relied on this method for going to the cinema:

You'd find a side way, you'd wait for somebody to come out of the back door, say "Give us your ticket guv'nor", get their ticket and duck in. Then you were crawling on your hands and knees so the attendant didn't see you.

Cinemas were still a novelty in 1900 but spread rapidly until there were some 4,500 in 1917. Originally called the "cinematograph" or "biograph", moving pictures had started in the 1890s as an ending to a music hall performance. The early films were jerky and covered with spots. Comic films and wild-west films became popular. Empty shops fitted with tip-up seats were the first real cinemas, but cinematograph-theatres were built from about 1906 on. Most early films were American and the audiences were largely schoolchildren. The films, of course, were silent, accompanied by the music of the piano-player in the theatre itself. Captions on the screen posed a prob-

50 Early 1900s. Punch and Judy shows were one of the many street entertainments.

lem for the many adults who could not read. Often children were taken along to read these captions aloud as they appeared.

Theatres too thrived in Edwardian times, and light-hearted family entertainment was most popular. The popular music of the time was mainly that which was heard in large music halls and in musical comedies.

Music and dancing

Street musicians were very much a part of Edwardian cities. In some areas children danced in the street. Cedric Fyson (b.1903) enjoyed the German bands which played regularly in the streets, calling at houses for money:

Ours, I recall, came every Tuesday and the children always liked to listen to them. I used to go to the door and give our weekly donation of two pence. These German bands, of course, disappeared in 1914 when war broke out.

Much musical entertainment was made in the home by families themselves. Pianos were widespread in better-off working-class homes as well as in middle- and upper-class families. Margaret and Pam Steven's (b.1911 and 1908) mother played the piano and sang nursery rhymes. ("We had to stand one each side of her.") In Albert Edward's (b.1904) Welsh home they played other instruments as well:

One had a Jew's Harp. And when they had rib beef we used to save the bones and make "clappers".

For adolescents in a country area, one Saturday night entertainment might be dancing to a fiddle. In towns and cities there was a greater choice of music halls, cinemas, and church concerts and lantern shows. The "youth parade" of adolescent boys and girls walking up and down, eyeing each other, offered further entertainment in itself.

51 1908. The gramophone was very popular in working-class homes which could afford it. Radio was actually developed in Edwardian times but public broadcasts did not start until after the First World War.

More leisure

As average working-hours fell from 60 or 70 hours a week in the nineteenth century to about 54 hours in 1910, there was more time for leisure. People also had somewhat more money to spend on leisure activities, which were more various than before.

The seaside

Family holidays for the well-off usually meant some time by the sea. Margaret and Pam Steven (b.1911 and 1908):

We went to the seaside every single year for about a month, taking enormous trunks by train, with nanny, always. We would wear our normal dresses, mostly with long sleeves and petticoats. Over that, with everything tucked inside, we used to have these waders made of a very oil-clothy sort of material, either

52 1911. Holiday-makers on beaches mostly wore their everyday thick clothes and hat. Even for bathing, men wore long-legged, striped costumes and women too were modestly covered all over.

scarlet or yellow. On the seashore we never wore anything else. We never went swimming at that young age, just paddling — with nanny waiting to dry your feet the moment you stepped out of the water. We took a terraced house for the month. There were two sitting-rooms, one for nanny and the children and one for the grown-ups upstairs. The owner of the house would do all the cooking but my mother would say what food she wanted. We went on the beach every single morning, and my father and any other males from the party would go and play golf. Our mother and nanny sat solemnly on the beach all morning,

58

while we paddled. Then lunch, and always a rest after lunch.

Many working-class families could only afford to go for the day to a coastal town, in excursion trains at a special fare. Sunday school outings or school outings to a holiday farm were the only holidays many children had.

Birthdays and Christmas
Many children hardly noticed birthdays either. Florence Goddard (b.1892), among others, did not celebrate birthdays at all.

The first birthday present I ever had was when I was twenty-one.

Edith Storry (b.1894) had some celebration:

You'd have four or five kiddies in. There was no birthday cake, couldn't afford that. There were little round currant scones about the size of your hand. They used to open them and butter them, put a halfpenny in one, a penny in another. The lucky one got a sixpence.

Edith Storry's Christmas:

We used to hang our stockings up Christmas and New Year, because my father was a Scotsman. We got more on New Year's Eve than what we got on Christmas. Everything in my stocking came from a penny bazaar. There was nothing dearer than a penny: suite of furniture for a doll's house, a doll, some of the loveliest cut glass dishes, penny child's umbrella.

Florence Goddard (b.1892), who went into service at the age of 13, received as a present from the mistress of the house a dress-length of cloth.

53   1907. Girls wearing one sort of "paddlers" into which dresses were tucked to keep them dry. Other "waders" were made of waterproof material and had a bib in front.

54 1910. Many city children had little chance of a holiday or even of a day by the sea. This picture shows how Fulham Council in London tried to bring the seaside to the children by collecting sand from Ramsgate and flooding part of Fulham Park.

55 1912. London workhouse children washing up at a holiday camp at Canvey Island. By 1912 the workhouses held 280,000 paupers (the highest number ever). It was 1916 before workhouses ended. Many people had preferred prison.

56　An East End fair in London, 1912.

According to Dorothy Fyson (b.1909), Christmas decorations were "less lavish than today. I can only remember paper chains made by ourselves". There was no coloured wrapping paper. Pam and Margaret Steven (b.1908 and 1911):

Gifts were wrapped in dull brown paper, if wrapped at all .... Always at Christmas time we had to learn a carol. Then we had to stand outside Mummy and Daddy's bedroom with our stockings in our hand. We had to sing our carol before we were allowed to go in and show what we had in our stockings.

Fairs

There were, of course, bank holiday fairs and country fairs which children enjoyed. Mop Fairs or Hiring Fairs had a serious purpose as well. Young people wanting a job stood in a long row with some clue as to what sort of work they sought — for example, would-be shepherds carried a crook. Once employment for the year had been sorted out, the young people would go off to enjoy themselves. Some of these fairs went on as late as 1905 or 1906. Florence Goddard (b.1892) went to the Mop Fair in Gloucestershire during the first two weeks in October. There were stalls selling gingerbread and other goods and foods.

14 Scouting

In 1907 twenty boys took part in an experimental scout camp at Brownsea Island, near Poole in Dorset. By the late 1970s there were more than 14 million scouts in over one hundred countries.

The beginning of the scout movement
The original organizer of the scouting movement was Robert Baden-Powell. He was a soldier and had written a book for other soldiers called *Aids to Scouting*.

On returning to England in 1901 (from the war in South Africa) he discovered that his book was being used by youth organizations. The founder of the Boys' Brigade

57 1909. An early patrol of scouts. Baden-Powell wrote in *Scouting for Boys*: ''Every patrol is named after some animal, and each scout in it has to be able to make a cry of that animal in order to communicate with his pals, especially at night. Thus you may be 'the Wolves', the Curlews', 'the Eagles', or 'the Rats' if you like.''

CUTTING FIREWOOD FOR A COTTAGER.
Boy Scouts' Good Turns.   No. 2.

urged Baden-Powell to re-write the book especially for boys. Baden-Powell set up the Brownsea camp in 1907 in order to try out some ideas.

Arthur Primmer (b.1892) was one of the original Brownsea scouts. He was "overjoyed" when, as a teenager in the Boys' Brigade he was chosen to go along:

> In 1907 I had never seen a motor car. We went from Poole Quay to Brownsea in a small boat driven by steam. At that time camping generally was unheard of. Only soldiers slept under canvas. We spent a lovely ten days.

The scout movement spreads

In 1908 Baden-Powell's handbook *Scouting for Boys* was issued in fortnightly parts at fourpence each. It was a great success. A penny weekly magazine called *The Scout* was also started in that year.

58 This was one of a series of postcards issued by *The Scout* magazine in 1908-9, showing likely good turns which scouts could perform. Others in the series show: "Wheeling an Old Man's Barrow up a Hill", "Mending a Farmer's Fence", "Scattering Sand in front of a Cart on a Slippery Road", "Carrying a Baby for a Tired Mother", "Putting a Stone under the Wheel of a Cart to Give the Horse a Rest".

When the Boy Scout movement was started, it was meant to be absorbed by existing boys' organizations such as the YMCA, the Boys' Brigade, the Church Lads' Brigade and the Jewish Lads' Brigade. But the movement grew quickly outside existing organizations. A headquarters was set up to co-ordinate the various groups of scouts which were being formed all over the country.

By 1909 the movement was flourishing. *Scouting for Boys* had been translated into five languages. Sea Scouts were formed.

Their handbook was written by Baden-Powell's elder brother, an ex-sailor. Over 11,000 scouts attended a Scout Rally held at the Crystal Palace in London. Baden-Powell saw there a group of girls who had formed a troop and he enrolled them as the first Girl Guides. By 1910 over 100,000 scouts had joined troops all over Britain.

Good turns

P.B. Nevill published a book in 1960 called *My Scouting Story* about his early years as a scout leader. He described how at his first meeting in 1909 there were two scout-masters present and only one boy! However, the next week six more boys came. Nevill says that there was much emphasis on doing good turns for other people — sometimes with embarrassing results. One scout heard the local gossip about a wife being unfaithful. He decided that his good turn would be to check up on this and inform the husband — whose wrath came down on Nevill for invasion of privacy. Scouts generally performed somewhat safer good turns, such as helping old women to cross the street.

Scout virtues

Besides urging a good turn every day, Baden-Powell's book emphasized that scouts should learn outdoor camping skills. Nevill reports that for his troop a five-mile walk over to Epping Forest for a scouting game and a five-mile walk back was not uncommon. When they went camping they would pile the bell-tents and kitbags on to a trek cart (an old builder's cart bought for £2). They would haul this by hand an average of ten miles a day, pitching the tents each night and packing them up again in the morning.

The scout movement encouraged all kinds of skills and virtues in young people. The 1911 requirement for a First Class Scout to have a "shilling in the savings bank" was meant to encourage thrift. *The Scout* magazine gave tips on such matters as pulling up stumps and how to stop a runaway horse. But the strongest emphasis was on patriotism. This was in keeping with the mood of the time. Baden-Powell urged in *Scouting for Boys*:

> Don't be disgraced like the young Romans who lost the Empire of their forefathers by being wishy-washy slackers without any go or patriotism in them.

When the war came, the scouts contributed to the war effort in many ways. For example, the Sea Scouts took the place of regular coastguards, which freed the men for service. What had been recreation and play became for real.

15 The War Comes

Albert Edwards (b.1904 in Wales) was ten years old when the First World War started. He used to go down to the town to sell newspapers:

> I'll always remember when they come out shouting "England Declares War on Germany". I was running around the streets with that, getting myself sixpence a night. You sold out in no time. There was no wireless then.

Edmund Dalton (b.1909 in Ireland):

> We used to lie in the fields and imagine that we could hear the big guns from France.

For Margaret and Pam Steven (b.1911 and 1908) living in Birmingham the coming of the war meant that they hardly saw their father. He worked away in London at the Ministry of Munitions (". . . the excitement of him coming back at week-ends"). For many children, fathers and older brothers away at the war were never seen again. The loss of life was higher than in any other war. Nearly 10 per cent of Edwardian men under 45 were killed, and another 20 per cent wounded.

With so many men away, women were needed in factories and offices. This meant that many more women were working outside the home, and many children too found themselves quickly drawn into the wider world. In some counties the official school-leaving age was temporarily reduced

59   1903. A well-to-do boy is dressed in uniform to have his photo taken. When the First World War started some eleven years later he would have been old enough to wear it for real. By 1915 the rapidly rising casualties left the nation stunned. Many more British men were killed in the First World War than in the Second World War.

60 **1914. A country walk in Yorkshire. The Great War of 1914-18 burst upon Britain and meant many social changes — simpler clothing, less drunkenness, freer love relationships.**

from 14 to 11. Four times as many children as before under the age of 14 found themselves at work. Schooling suffered much disruption.

Unemployment went up at first, but by late 1916 the need for workers in war production meant that many poorer families were in some ways better off than before 1914. Many young men in uniform were better fed as soldiers than they had been in pre-war years.

Edwardians alive today remember as children queueing for sugar, potatoes and other foodstuffs that were short. Edmund Dalton (b.1909 in Ireland):

You didn't get the white flour in the bread. So the bread was darker, much darker.

Most important were not the temporary shortages and disruptions but the social changes which carried on after the war. Children and young people felt the increasing freedoms, the breakdown of the old country house system and the move away from domestic service jobs. These and other changes marked the end of an era.

Glossary

anaemic	having undernourished blood, causing tiredness
Board Schools	schools set up by School Boards in late nineteenth century
calico	white cotton cloth
Children's Charter	collection of reforms and new laws to help children in early twentieth century
crofter	someone who farms a small enclosed field, usually by a house
Empire Day	24 May, holiday to celebrate the British Empire
Garden City	planned development of houses, shops, workplaces built to combine advantages of both town and country life
gramophone	early record player
half-time system	system whereby children worked half the day in a factory or field, and went to school for the other half day
hansom cabs	two-wheeled cab holding two people inside, driver up behind holding reins of horse
hops	ripened cones of female hop-plants, used for flavouring malt liquors
horse omnibuses	horse-pulled, four-wheeled public vehicle with seats on roof as well as inside
jack	vessel for holding liquid
knickerbockers	loose-fitting trousers, gathered in at the knee
lather boys	boys who worked for barbers, covering faces with foam in readiness to be shaved
liberty bodice	undergarment worn by girls
Mop Fairs	country fairs used for finding hired help as well as for enjoyment
paddlers	large waterproof pants worn over skirts by girls at the seaside
papier mâché	paper reduced to a pulp and moulded
pauper	very poor person with no means of livelihood
pinafore	white sleeveless covering worn by girls over dresses
rickets	disease causing softening of bones and bow legs, caused by vitamin deficiency
Standard	class in a British elementary school
suffragette	female campaigner for votes for women
tramcars	public carriages running on rails
workhouses	unpleasant places where poor, ill and old were housed in exchange for work done

ACKNOWLEDGMENTS

The author warmly thanks the following for contributing personal memories to this book:

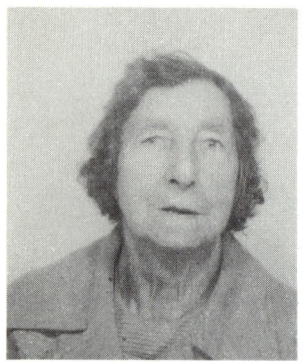

Flo Connors
(b. 1901)

Edmund Dalton
(b. 1909)

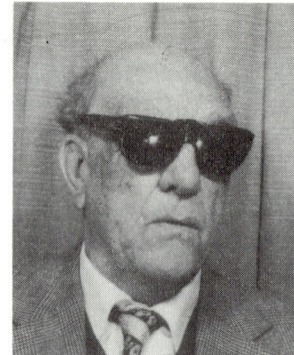

Albert Edwards
(b. 1904)

Dorothy Fyson
(b. 1909)

Cedric Fyson
(b. 1903)

Cedric Fyson at age 13 in 1916

Florence Goddard
(b. 1892)

Frances Hillsdon
(b. 1908)

Fred Hillsdon
(b. 1906)

**Lulu Lee
(b. 1889)**

**Arthur Primmer
(b. 1892)**

**Margaret Steven
(b. 1911)**

**Pam (Steven) Hearn
(b. 1908)**

Pam (Steven) Hearn at age 3 in 1911

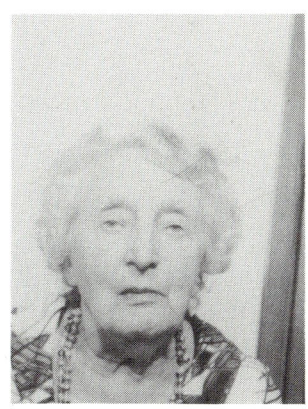

**Edith Storry
(b. 1894)**

Appreciation also to the following: P. Cooke of the Scout Association, the Sheen Lane Day Centre, and Kathleen Goddard. The Author and Publishers would like to thank the following for their kind permission to reproduce copyright illustrations in the book: BBC Hulton Picture Library for frontispiece and figs 1-21, 23, 25, 26, 28-35, 37-45, 47-57, 59, 60; the Mansell Collection for figs 22, 24, 27, 36, 46; The Scout Association Archive for fig 58.

Books for Further Reading

Non-fiction

You can get more information about the Edwardian period and the way people lived then from:

Cecil, Robert, *Life in Edwardian England*, Batsford, 1969
Fisher, John, *The World of the Forsytes*, Secker & Warburg, 1976
Hardwick, Mollie, *The World of Upstairs, Downstairs*, David & Charles, 1976
McMillan, James, *The Way We Were* 1900-1914, William Kimber, 1978
Middlemas, Keith, *The Life and Times of Edward VII*, Weidenfeld and Nicolson, 1972
Norton, Graham, *London Before the Blitz* 1906-1940, Macdonald, 1970
Pearsall, *Edwardian Life and Leisure*, David & Charles, 1973
Priestley, J.B., *The Edwardians*, Heinemann, 1970
Thompson, Paul, *The Edwardians*, Weidenfeld and Nicolson, 1975
Thompson, Paul and Harkell, Gina, *The Edwardians in photographs*, Batsford, 1979

Autobiography

There are many books by people who were young in Edwardian times, telling about their early lives. Here are just a few titles:

Burnett, J., *Useful Toil*, 1974 (collection of working-class auto-
  biographies)
Keppel, Sonia, *Edwardian Daughter*, 1959
Roberts, Robert, *The Classic Slum*, 1971

Fiction

A few good novels about Edwardian life and times are:

Forster, E.M., *Howard's End*, 1910
Galsworthy, J., *The Forsyte Saga*, 1906-21
James, Henry, *The Golden Bowl*, 1904
Wells, H.G., *The History of Mr. Polly*, 1910

Index

The numbers in **bold type** refer to the figure numbers of illustrations and/or picture captions